AFTER LOSS

Hope for Widows, Widowers,
and Partners

LINDA DONOVAN

authorHOUSE®

AuthorHouse™
1663 Liberty Drive
Bloomington, IN 47403
www.authorhouse.com
Phone: 1 (800) 839-8640

This publication is designed to educate and provide general information regarding the subject material covered. It is not intended to replace the counsel of other professional advisers such as doctors, psychologists, lawyers, or financial planners. Readers are encouraged to consult with their own advisers regarding specific situations. While the author has taken reasonable precautions in the preparation of this book and believes the facts presented within the book are accurate, the author assumes no responsibility for errors or omissions. The author specifically disclaims any liability resulting from the use or application of the information contained in this book. The information within this book is not intended to serve as emotional or therapeutic advice related to individual situations.

Names and identifying details have been changed to protect the privacy of individuals.

Published by AuthorHouse 08/29/2019

ISBN: 978-1-7283-2099-1 (sc)
ISBN: 978-1-7283-2097-7 (hc)
ISBN: 978-1-7283-2098-4 (e)

Library of Congress Control Number: 2019910873

Print information available on the last page.

Certain stock imagery © Getty Images.

Author photo by Della Calfee

This book is printed on acid-free paper.

PRAISE FOR *AFTER LOSS*

▼

"Goes to where you are, accepts it, and takes you forward from there with compassion and support. It's like talking with a loving and comforting friend who completely understands what you're going through."

—Deborah Malkin, Attorney at Law, Certified Specialist in Estate Planning, Trusts, and Probate

"Grieving created many obstacles that made it difficult to move on after my wife's death. This book shows how to overcome them by providing solid strategies with real-life examples. The book made me realize that I was not alone with my feelings and fears and identified a pathway with achievable goals to support the healing process."

—Paul Karz

"Contains valuable and practical insights for anyone coping with loss. The author is clearly an expert and becomes a trusted friend throughout the pages. Highly recommended."

—Alesa Lightbourne, Ph.D., Author of *The Kurdish Bike*

"Sometimes you have no choice in the path life takes you. As a widow, I know that you often have choices once you are on that path. That is to make plans, survive, and find happiness. Make good choices, don't be afraid to investigate options, and do the hard tasks to make yourself financially independent. This book offers guidance to set you on the right path."

—Patti Schlunt

CONTENTS

To my family with love and gratitude. To the memory of Paul (my late husband), Lenny (my dad), Shelly (my stepfather), and Kelly (my friend).

INTRODUCTION

▼

It takes a lot of work to put your life back together after a loss. You may wonder why you're still feeling stuck, lonely, or struggling, even if it has been a year or many years since your spouse or partner died. To complicate matters, you may not be sure how to deal with the seemingly unrelenting financial, emotional, legal, physical, and logistical obstacles you face. This book will help you learn how to tackle those challenges, answer some of your most pressing questions about moving forward, and help you to get back on your feet again.

How do you know when you're ready to rebuild your life after loss? I had a defining moment that motivated me. I had never lived alone until my daughter, Laura, left home to attend college several months after my husband, Paul, died. It was a shock adjusting to an empty house with no one to keep me company except my Jack Russell terrier, Roxy. Since I worked from my home, I spent more time with my dog than I did with people.

One night, as Roxy sat upright in a chair at the dinner table, I stared at her, watching closely as she eagerly waited for me to put scraps of chicken on her plate. She nodded her head, looked at me straight in the eyes, and carefully put her paw up and down on the table repeatedly. This was her way of asking me for a second helping. I suddenly realized that there was something very wrong with this picture. Although I loved my dog, I needed to spend more time with people. I was ready to move outside my comfort zone. The key was in figuring out how to get started.

You might have experienced a similar time when your grief shifted. The approach you use in tending to your grief may vary, based on your age, your support network, economic situation, or gender. It can be influenced by where you live, how the person died, unresolved issues that need to be addressed, complex family/ stepfamily situations, and other factors. *After Loss* describes how to take these circumstances into consideration, create a plan that works best for you, and implement it at a comfortable pace.

I can relate to loss because I've gone through it. The recommendations in this book are based on my own experience as a widow and Paul's caretaker, along with an understanding of modern best practices for grief support. I've led grief groups for Hospice of Santa Cruz County, providing support to widows, widowers, partners, and their families for more than ten years. From firsthand experience, I also understand the impact that loss can have on the children of the deceased. These experiences have enabled me to help many people cope with loss and issues related to family dynamics. I've helped them to find fulfillment in their lives and relationships.

Although the path to rebuilding your life may seem frustrating and overwhelming at times, you can emerge from this experience with resilience and insight you never expected. You can take steps that will be comforting, practical, and rewarding over time. *After Loss* will be your guide to help you take control.

Keep in mind that when you lose the one you love, your own identity changes. I'll show you how to cope with the "new normal" and help you to develop goals, expand your horizons, make informed decisions, and nurture relationships with others. You'll discover how to define who you are and what you want. Perhaps you'll pursue a rewarding hobby or career.

In fact, you might even find a new companion or fall in love again. Although the prospect of entering into a new relationship may be the furthest thing from your mind now, it could happen someday. So be open to new possibilities. I did and found happiness again, just like some of the other people that you'll read about in this book.

EVERYONE SHOULD READ THE APPENDIX. *IF YOUR LOSS HAS BEEN RECENT—WITHIN THE LAST YEAR—I SUGGEST THAT YOU READ THE APPENDIX FIRST.* THE APPENDIX DESCRIBES THE GRIEF PROCESS AND INCLUDES STRATEGIES FOR GETTING THROUGH THE FIRST YEAR. THEN, READ THE FIRST TWO CHAPTERS, WHICH WILL HELP YOU TO WORK THROUGH THE TASKS OF GRIEF AND DEVELOP APPROACHES FOR MOVING FORWARD.

IN SOME CASES, IT MIGHT BE MANY MONTHS BEFORE YOU'RE PREPARED TO FOCUS ON THE OTHER CHAPTERS, BUT KEEP THIS BOOK HANDY SO THAT IT'S AVAILABLE WHEN THE TIME IS RIGHT.

Although *After Loss* doesn't replace professional help, it's designed to provide you with comfort and tools to assist you throughout your grief journey. The stories of people you'll read about are composites based on real-world scenarios. They're about people dealing with many of the challenges you might experience. They don't refer to any specific individuals, except where I've clearly indicated that some were my family members or friends.

These questions may help you to define if you're ready to move forward with the next stage of rebuilding your life. You'll find out how to address them and explore many other topics of interest in *After Loss.*

- Are you interested in discovering who you really are and what you want, now that your role has changed?
- Would you like to learn ways to deal with everyday challenges?
- Do you have the energy to make some changes?
- Have you thought about what it takes to declutter your home or life?
- Do you know how to get the emotional, logistical, and financial support you might need?

- Are you interested in going back to work or engaging in social activities but don't know how to get started?
- Do you need help dealing with family dynamics?
- Are you struggling with deciding where to live?
- Would you like to identify and set some achievable goals to improve the quality of your life and find joy?
- Have you figured out some of the best ways to avoid loneliness and isolation?
- If you're interested in dating or companionship, do you know how to pursue it in a way that's most comfortable for you?

Let this book be your road map to adjusting to your new life and helping you to achieve fulfillment, hope, and joy again. I found it, and so can you.

(In case you are wondering how Roxy handled the change in her status, she was much happier—even though she was banned from the dinner table—as I became stronger and more self-assured.)

CHAPTER 1

▼

WORKING THROUGH THE
TASKS OF GRIEF

How many times have you heard someone ask, "When are you going to stop grieving?" It's a common, unsettling statement. People who say this don't realize that tending to grief is a journey, and it takes time to adapt. If you start crying when you hear a song because it reminds you of your partner, or you are uncomfortable in social situations where everyone else is coupled and seems happy, you're not alone.

Perhaps you can't even go back to restaurants where you had meals with your loved one. That reaction is perfectly normal. If you cry at your son's wedding, your daughter's graduation, or your grandson's birth because your husband isn't there to enjoy it, understand that this type of response is common.

Hospice refers to the process of tending to grief as "doing grief work." And it is work! No one grieves in the same way as anyone else; there's no one-size-fits-all template. Fortunately, you can use a variety of strategies to help ease the pain and enable you to move forward with your life. In this chapter, I'll discuss some of them and give you tools for moving at the pace that works best for you.

JOURNALING YOUR WAY THROUGH LOSS

Even if your partner was terminally ill and you expected his death, it's still a difficult adjustment in moving from *we* to *me*. One the most effective tools for coping, which has helped many people, involves journaling, whether it's done early after a loss, over a period of many months, or much longer.

This approach was easy for me to follow and maintain. I made it a practice to write down my feelings each night for the first few months after Paul's death. Paul died of cancer that spread to his liver almost six months after he was diagnosed. I set aside a certain time each day that was exclusively devoted to working through my grief by journaling. I continued to write in my journal on an occasional basis more than a year after his passing.

Although I didn't realize it then, that routine helped me to handle my daily responsibilities more effectively because it gave me time to focus on grief outside of my working hours. I was working full time and taking care of my teenage daughter when Paul died. Journaling was my private time to communicate with Paul and reflect upon how I was going to manage without him.

I had several other daily rituals that were comforting. Each night at 10:30, before I went to sleep, I would write a letter to him and describe my day and emotions. I'd go through the usual conversations that I might have had with him if he had been alive. At times, my letters were very sad. I'd ask him questions like, "Why did you have to die so soon?" I'd describe the day's events, whether it involved telling him about my accomplishing a major goal at work or how the Boston Red Sox had fared that day. He was a big Red Sox fan, and one of the last things he said to me while he was still able to speak was, "Did the Red Sox win the big game?" Even when they lost, I would tell him the Red Sox were doing fine. After all, why upset a dying man who has worshipped his favorite team his entire life?

One of the benefits of journaling is that it gives you the opportunity to communicate with your loved ones and ask any questions that you may not have asked during their lifetimes. This helps you cope with unfinished business.

Also, if you have any regrets, you can share them in your journal. If you regret that you didn't do enough to prevent the death (even if there was nothing you could have done), go ahead and write this in the journal. It's a chance for you to get your feelings out of your head and onto paper, where they can be shared. Then these words no longer will be in the back of your mind when you're supposed to be mentally present somewhere else. You're essentially freeing up space in your brain, like offloading memory to a flash drive, so that you can focus on moving forward.

You might ask, "What good is journaling if the communication is only one way?" Here's why it's so important: you can actually get answers to your questions. That's right—the next part of journaling is to put yourself in your partner's shoes and see how he or she would respond. Here's what a typical letter might look like:

Jim,

I'm sorry that I couldn't do anything to stop you from having a heart attack. I called 911, but you died before they arrived at the hospital. If only I'd been in the garage when you were there and had the attack, I could have saved you. But how was I to know you were in danger? I feel so guilty, and I miss you more than you'll ever know. I can't stop thinking that if I had put my book down and checked on you in the garage before this happened, you'd be here today. I feel like it's all my fault. How will I ever get through this nightmare?

Maria

Now, it's time for Maria to dig deep down into her memory and write a new letter to herself, this time from Jim's perspective.

Maria,

Sometimes things happen that are well beyond our control. You had no reason to believe that I was having a heart attack. Everything occurred so quickly. In fact, I didn't know I was experiencing a heart attack either. There wasn't anything that you or anyone could have done to help me.

I love you so much and want you to know how happy I was to have spent my life with you. I want the best for you. Please enjoy each moment for me, and know that I will always be with you in your memories.

Love,
Jim

Think about the value of this exercise and the power of journaling. Things that you wish could be said are expressed. By writing in Jim's voice, Maria was able to put her mind at ease with the comforting thoughts that he would convey to her. As a result, she was able to stop replaying in her mind the nightmare of that awful evening.

Journaling is one of a variety of ways to communicate with yourself, to help resolve issues that are troubling you, and to still feel connected to your loved one. What I found most interesting when I went back and looked at the journal entries in the first few months following Paul's death was that I became much more practical and outwardly sane as time progressed.

My initial entries contained messages of despair. Gradually, they became more conversational, to the point where I described what was happening in politics, how I managed to fixed a broken washing machine all by myself, and how our favorite TV series ended. Eventually, I cut back on journaling as I became more focused on the world around me and the tasks needed to rebuild my life.

FINDING OTHER WAYS TO COMMUNICATE

If you don't like to write in a journal, consider other types of expression. Some people routinely talk to their loved ones out loud and then think about how their partners would respond. Others convey their feelings through prayer or meditation. Some people enjoy creating artwork to release their emotions. For example, painting a picture, building something with clay, or making a collage are practical ways to get in touch with your emotions around grief. A friend of mine communicated her anger about cancer by throwing paint against a canvas to create an image that portrayed a tumor out of control. She even won an award for the painting, which ultimately was displayed in an art gallery.

One woman wrote songs for her husband and played them on her guitar. Another woman planted a garden in her partner's honor and went there daily to connect with him and discuss what was on her mind. Some people play videos of their deceased loved ones and then talk to them as if they are still in the room.

If you're having problems making decisions, particularly those that you made with your loved one, ask yourself, *What would my partner want me to do in this situation?* Ask your questions at the end of the day, when you're less likely to encounter any distractions. Then let the answers come to you.

Here's an example:

It was just before Christmas when Denise's daughter, Elaine, who had a new baby, split up with her husband. Elaine's husband demanded that she return the wedding ring he'd given her. Denise, who had lost her own husband five years earlier, was worried that Elaine would be distraught over the breakup. At the same time, Denise wondered what she could do to make Elaine feel better.

Denise shouted out loud to her departed husband. "Sam, I need you to tell me how to help Elaine. What can I do?" She sat patiently waiting for some guidance and looked at her hands, and the answer became clear. The wedding ring that Sam (Elaine's father) had given to Denise had been moved to her middle finger years ago. The ring obviously held sentimental value to Denise, which is why she continued to wear it, but not on her wedding finger. Yet it occurred to her that Elaine really needed the ring. Denise felt that she was guided by Sam to give the ring to Elaine, which she did. Elaine proudly wore the ring in memory of her father, and it helped cheer her up at a difficult time.

KEEPING A MOOD DIARY TO SUPPORT SELF-CARE

In grief groups, we put a lot of emphasis on self-care—encouraging you to do something that makes you happy, be gentle with yourself, limit the number of decisions you make at a given time, maintain a regular schedule, and so on.

Keeping a mood diary is different from journaling, and it's easy to do. Use this diary to identify what causes you stress or pain and what helps you to feel comfortable. If you can find and track what triggers certain moods, you can create a plan to provide better self-care. Here's how to get started:

Mood Diary Guidelines

1. Keep a notebook, and have each page in the notebook represent a day.

2. Each day, when you experience something uncomfortable, write it down. It doesn't have to be long. It could be a short sentence.
3. Also write down what made you happy.
4. At the end of the day, write down any insights this process has given you.

Here's what a mood diary entry might look like for one day.

- I called Susan, and it was frustrating talking with her. She expects more of me than I can give. This made me sad and angry.
- I took a walk and enjoyed looking at the trees in the park.
- The man who was supposed to fix my dishwasher never showed up. It got me really upset. I have enough problems without people flaking out on me.
- I liked watching my favorite show on TV.
- Insight: I'll contact Susan less frequently because it gets me upset when I have to deal with her. She's a relative, and I know she means well, but I don't have the energy to spend much time with her right now. I'll plan to walk more often in the park. I'll call someone else to fix the dishwasher when I have time. I'll watch my favorite TV show when it's convenient and I need a break.

It's amazing what you'll learn when you start tracking patterns that lead to ups and downs. If you didn't keep a mood diary, you might not realize how to cope with the impact that Susan has on you or how walking and watching your favorite TV show provides the breaks you need to help deal with stress. After keeping a diary for about a month, you should have a good idea of what can help positively impact your moods, and you can make changes that lead to feeling better.

If you don't have time to keep a formal mood diary, then just jot down notes on a small sticky pad. List what happened, how it made you feel, and the date. Put that note on a large piece of paper. Look at the sticky-pad notes after a week or so, and see if there are common patterns in what makes you happy or sad.

ADDRESSING UNFINISHED BUSINESS: ANGER, GUILT, AND FORGIVENESS

It's very common to feel tremendous guilt about something you did or didn't do to help your loved ones. There might be something you wanted to tell your spouse or partner but never had the chance. You might also be angry at others. Writing a letter to help you deal with this unfinished business can be helpful and liberating. It's also a way to forgive yourself, your deceased partner or spouse, and whoever else you think might have contributed to the loss.

Unfinished Business Exercise

Set aside about thirty minutes or more of quiet, uninterrupted time in a peaceful setting to collect your thoughts. Complete these sentences to help articulate what's on your mind.

Message to Your Spouse or Partner

1. I love you because …
2. I'm angry at you because …
3. I forgive you because …
4. One thing I would like to say that I never got to tell you is …
5. If I could change anything I've said or done, it would be …

Message to Yourself

6. I feel guilty because …
7. I forgive myself because …
8. I'm angry at others because …

9. I forgive those people because …

The following example can help you to understand how to write this letter:

> Debbie was devastated because her partner, Pat, died in a car accident on the way to the grocery store late at night. Pat had decided to pick up dessert for the two of them. Debbie had told Pat not to go to the store because it was late, raining hard, the streets were flooded, and Pat had drunk a few glasses of wine earlier in the evening. Pat was determined and decided to go anyway. On his way to the store, the road visibility was poor, and Pat crashed his car into a tree. He was rushed to hospital, but despite efforts by doctors and nurses, Pat's injuries were too extensive. He died.
>
> Writing the letter wasn't easy. Still, it was important for Debbie to express her emotions because it was becoming increasingly difficult to concentrate and stay in the present moment. When she watched TV, her mind would wander and repeat everything that had happened on that horrible night and how the accident could have been prevented. As a result, she was unable remember very much about the TV programs she saw.
>
> The same thoughts about that night kept jumping into her head when she'd have conversations with friends and would lose track of what they were saying. When Debbie ate meals, she was so stressed that she stopped enjoying the taste of her favorite foods. Here's what her letter looked like:

Message to Pat

I love you because we shared a wonderful life together and have so many great memories. We raised a family, traveled the world, laughed at each other's jokes, and encouraged each other to be successful in our careers. We had many friends and enjoyed simple pleasures, like walking through the woods, reading the newspaper together while having breakfast, and watching our children grow up to be independent. We had such fascinating conversations that I always thought of you as the most interesting man in the world.

Our holidays were very special. Every Thanksgiving you got up at 6:00 a.m. to put the turkey in the oven and make it just perfect so that our family could enjoy a wonderful feast. You took care of me when I was sick and put our family needs first. Your hugs and kisses were loving, and I treasured them just as I cherished you.

I'm angry at you because I told you not to leave that night. I urged you to stay in, especially since you'd drunk a few glasses of wine, and the weather was so bad. But you didn't listen to me. Getting dessert was more important to you than your life! Now I'm here alone, and I feel like you abandoned me. I can't bear to be without you.

> "Now I'm here alone, and I feel like you abandoned me. I can't bear to be without you."

Yet you were so stubborn that you didn't do what I asked. If only you had listened to me, you'd still be here!

I forgive you because you had no idea that going to the grocery store would lead to this tragedy. It was wrong for you to drive after having two glasses of wine, but the alcohol didn't seem to have affected you. Besides, we had the drinks three hours before you left. When they did a blood-alcohol test on you at the hospital, the results showed it was at a safe level. The police report indicated that anyone driving in that area at night during a such bad storm likely would have experienced the same deadly outcome.

If there's one thing I would like to say that I never got to tell you, it would be that I'm sorry for all of the times I complained about petty things you did that sometimes annoyed me. I wish had been more understanding because I miss you so much, and I now think of your quirks as endearing.

If I could change anything I've said or done, it would be to have spent more time with you and worked less. I can't get that time back, now that you're gone.

Message to Herself

I feel guilty because I didn't try harder to prevent you from leaving. If only I had given you an ultimatum and been more forceful in stopping you from going to the store. While I didn't want you to go, I also wanted the dessert. So I feel like it's my fault.

I forgive myself because I didn't know you would get into an accident. You'd driven to that store hundreds of times. It was only two miles away. Sometimes things are out of our control. The accident happened, and it's not my fault.

I'm angry at others because the city should've had more lights on the street. It was dark. The doctors and nurses should've done something more to save you. I don't know what it is that could've made a difference, but I'm mad that they were unable to prevent your death. I'm mad at God for letting this happen. You were only fifty years old and didn't deserve this. All of our life plans have been disrupted. How could God let this happen?

I forgive everyone I just blamed because many roads are dimly lit. It's not the city's fault. I read the medical reports and talked with the doctors and nurses. They truly tried their best. Their job is to save lives. As far as God goes, sometimes bad things happen, and there's no way to explain it. But if I stay angry, it's going to drain me. There's nothing I can do to change what happened, so I'll just have to accept it and stop being obsessed with negative thoughts.

Writing this letter helped Debbie to release her feelings of guilt, cope with unfinished business, forgive others, and set herself free.

Many religions help people cope with loss and other personal challenges by reinforcing the power of forgiveness. When you can understand what's making you angry and forgive the people and circumstances that you think may have contributed to these negative emotions, you can free up energy. Then you can make room for resilience, strength, and the desire to pursue what makes you happy. By communicating anything you would've liked to have shared with your loved one, you're helping to resolve any unfinished business.

GETTING HELP WITH GRIEF SUPPORT AND THERAPY

When you lose a spouse or partner, your social circle may change, particularly if most of your friends are couples. I lived in a suburban community, and nearly all of my friends were married. It has now been about thirteen years since Paul died, and my married friends in the old neighborhood remain very close to me to this day. These people and my family played a key role in helping me get through the trauma of being a widow at age fifty-four. Other friends that I have known most of my life also were there for me through this crisis, even though many of them lived a plane flight away.

While I had a great support network—loving children, their spouses, stepchildren, my mom, Paul's wonderful family, other relatives, a great neighborhood, and long-term friends—I needed more. This involved expanding my support network to include some people who were single. Some of these new friends were widows, and others were divorced.

I also needed grief support to help understand how to cope after losing my husband about thirty years sooner than I had ever anticipated. I began by getting some one-on-one help from Hospice of Santa Cruz County. This type of service might also be available from your local hospice, even if your spouse or partner wasn't under the care of hospice when that person died.

My individual sessions were with a trained grief-support volunteer for about an hour, once a week. In these sessions, I discussed what had happened during the week, my concerns, and any upcoming issues. The volunteer listened and helped to normalize what I was going through and gave me some guidance to make life easier.

While I'm a strong advocate of grief groups, you may not be ready to enter a group session right away. You may initially find one-on-one support is more valuable in the beginning. This is particularly common in cases where the loss is so great and traumatic that individual support can be more comforting than sharing your grief story in a group setting, at least until you're ready.

When I finished the individual sessions, I attended a grief group focused on the loss of a spouse or partner. It provided an excellent opportunity to learn how to deal with grief and to develop some new friendships.

The group gave me the chance to discuss my loss with people who truly understood what I was going through. I could do this in a safe, nonjudgmental place. It made me feel that I was not alone. As difficult as my situation was at the time, I realized that other people suffered so much more.

Instead of feeling sorry for myself, I began to appreciate how lucky I was to have a support system because many people were completely on their own. I had loving children, stepchildren, a daughter-in-law, and a new grandchild on the way. My mom, stepfather, and Paul's family offered guidance through the years. Plus, I loved my job, which gave me the resources to support my daughter and myself and helped to provide a structure for my daily routines.

By attending the grief group, I was able to learn more about the grief process. It helped me to accept the loss and included a variety of exercises to explore what I needed to do to eventually rebuild my life. These group meetings made me feel better because the sessions made me realize that my reactions to grief were common. As a result, I felt less scared and alone.

> I also met a dear friend, Angie, who lost her husband around the same time I did. Her loss was very tragic—a sudden heart attack. Our children were about the same age, we had a lot in common, and we made it a point to meet once a week for dinner, which we did for many years. Angie and I called this "friend therapy."
>
> It was really helpful getting to know Angie, and I still consider her one of my closest friends. We went on trips together and comforted each other during our own challenges as they arose over time. I'm sure that we will be friends forever and will always stay in touch.

Ultimately, I felt compelled to give back to the organization that had done so much to help me and my family. I thought that if I could be trained to lead grief groups and work one-on-one to help others heal, then something positive could result from Paul's death. I had benefitted from the grief group and one-on-one sessions I attended at my local hospice. I was wiser, more caring, humbled by the loss, and ready to give back to the organization that had helped my family.

Fortunately, I was accepted into the volunteer grief-support program of Hospice of Santa Cruz County, and my involvement with hospice had a profound positive impact on my life in many ways. In 2008, almost two years after Paul's passing, I went through grief-support training. I continue to participate in the ongoing professional development sessions hospice offers and to lead grief groups.

This volunteer work became very personally rewarding. I also made new friends with some of the other people who supported hospice in various capacities. (One of those friends, in fact, invited me to an event where I met a wonderful man, Jack, in 2015. Jack and I got married a few years later. I never thought it would be possible to love someone so deeply again. He captured my heart, and I'm forever grateful to have found him.)

Your grief-support volunteer or counselor may recommend other resources to help you. Some situations, based on the type of loss and an individual's own circumstances, may be helped by seeing a licensed therapist or psychiatrist. Remember, you don't have to deal with your grief alone, even if you don't have a family, your good friends live far away, or you feel totally isolated. There are many community services available, regardless of your income. Call or visit your local city community center online to learn more about their resources.

WONDERING WHY YOU'RE GRIEVING IF YOU WERE IN AN UNHAPPY RELATIONSHIP

Many people in grief groups or who get counseling are there because they're devastated that they've lost their spouses or partners and can't imagine being without them. Some people, however, are grieving, and they don't know why. They may have been in very unhappy or unhealthy relationships that they stayed in because it was just too much effort to leave. Perhaps they felt sorry for their spouses (even though they no longer were in love with them), or they couldn't afford financially to leave the relationship. They may have completely grown apart but remained a couple for the sake of their children.

When they attend grief groups, it may be difficult because they're sad and often "stuck," but they don't miss their deceased partner. And they tend to feel guilty about having those emotions when others express true love for the person who died. Here's the catch: even if your relationship was rocky and even if you feel a bit relieved that you don't have to deal with that person anymore, there are a number of reasons why you're grieving. Grief support can help you too.

Here are some reasons to consider:

1. You mourn what could have been. There was likely a time when you had a dream for your relationship and that it would work out successfully. Something initially attracted you to that person. When your partner or spouse is gone, you realize that it's too late to change things.
2. You mourn the old times, when the relationship was good. You feel guilty that you weren't able to make the relationship any better over time. Now it's too late.
3. You miss what's familiar. Your relationship was far from perfect, yet you may cling to what is known. Now that the structure of your life has changed, you'll likely deal with a lot of unknowns. You'll need to take risks to move forward, and you may not be ready to do that.
4. Your other family members and friends may be grieving, and you have to deal with their loss too. Perhaps you and your husband didn't get along with each other, but your children loved him and miss him. You may struggle with conflicted feelings of relief mixed with guilt and worry about how that impacts your relationships with other family members.
5. Your lifestyle may change and have a negative financial impact on you. If you stayed in an unhappy relationship but managed to maintain a lifestyle that was comfortable, you may find yourself having to relocate, scale back, or make other sacrifices to deal with financial pressures that arise. If you were a stepparent and your spouse, the breadwinner, left

everything to his or her kids, you may find yourself having to move out of the house where you're currently living and start over.

6. Your role has changed, and the responsibility is overwhelming. You and your spouse or partner may have drifted apart over the years, yet you stayed together because it was too much effort to maintain the household if you lived apart. Now you'll have to take over the things that person managed—taking care of the kids, planning activities, assuming full responsibility for family meal preparation, paying the bills, and so on.

7. You feel guilty about being relieved. Perhaps your spouse or partner had a substance abuse or alcohol problem that put a tremendous strain on the relationship. You wanted out of the relationship but didn't end it. When that person died, you were freed of the burden of never knowing what type of mood you would need to cope with when you arrived home from work. Would it be a good day or a bad one? You may be angry at yourself for feeling relieved.

If you find yourself grieving the loss of your spouse or partner, even though the relationship was often unpleasant, consider getting one-on-one grief support or the help of a therapist. While a grief group can be useful, individual assistance might make you feel more comfortable about moving forward and letting go of your self-critical or conflicted feelings.

KNOWING WHAT TO DO WHEN WHAT'S FAMILIAR IS NOT YOUR FRIEND—AT LEAST NOT RIGHT AWAY

When you were a couple, chances are you had a favorite restaurant, wonderful memories of places that you visited, and local shops that you went to on a regular basis. Going to these locations alone might be comforting, but in many cases, it can cause emotional stress that you hadn't anticipated. Be prepared for an unexpected reaction when you initially return to these places on your own. It may take time before you feel at ease in these settings. Here are some examples:

Before Paul was diagnosed with cancer, I remember our routine of going to the grocery store together after breakfast on Saturday mornings. At the time we had this weekly errand, I never thought of the experience of trudging through a grocery store as one that was particularly bonding or fun. It was just another chore to do on my day off from work. I went because he wanted me to join him, even though it always took twice as long when we did this together as when I shopped alone.

It wasn't until he died that I realized how much I missed our trips to the store. About two weeks after his death, I walked into the store with tears in my eyes, knowing that this simple routine would never be the same. I thought of all the times I grudgingly joined Paul, and I wished I had appreciated our time together. It was so lonely walking into that familiar place without him.

As I moved my cart across one of aisles, I heard a couple fighting with each other. I walked over to them and said, "Are you married?" When the wife answered yes, I looked this stranger in the eyes and said, "Both of you should stop fighting and hug instead. Be grateful that you have each other. I used to come shopping here every week with my husband, but I can't do that anymore because he just died."

The couple looked at me, speechless. Then they hugged each other and thanked me for reminding them of the importance of being together. Maybe after I left, they spoke about the crazy woman who had barged in on their conversation and told them what to do. Either way, it made me realize how much I missed the ordinary activities with Paul and that I needed to adjust to that change.

I decided to wait a few months before returning to that store again. It wasn't because I was embarrassed that I yelled at strangers. It was because I knew that I had to wait until I was comfortable walking in there alone. When I was finally emotionally able to return to the store, I made it a special point to avoid going there on Saturday mornings.

Several months after Paul died, my daughter went off to college. It was the first time I wanted to enjoy having a nice dinner at my favorite restaurant and was able to go there by myself. While this sounds like something that should be easy to do, it wasn't. Like many widows of my generation (baby boomers), I had always lived within someone—parents, roommates, a husband, and children.

I was fifty-four and realized that I had never lived alone! I brought a newspaper with me to the restaurant, ordered dinner, and even though I felt lonely being there without Paul, I got through the meal. I promised myself that if I ever visited any of our old favorite places and felt uneasy, I would just bring a friend instead of going there alone. Or I'd avoid those venues until I was ready. By the time I was prepared to go to places like that alone, I actually enjoyed the experience. I got to eat what I wanted, when I wanted, and sit quietly, reading a newspaper, which I found was very relaxing.

Now, think about what happens when you return to your favorite vacation locations without your spouse or partner. I loved Maui, and Paul I went there a few times together and had wonderful memories. Shortly after Paul died, my sons, Kevin and Michael, planned a trip to Maui. They used their frequent-flyer miles and got us hotel and flight reservations. I was so grateful that they had done this for me. It was such a loving gesture. Yes, Hawaii is for lovers, and I was worried about how I would react to being there without Paul. Being surrounded by my family, however, helped to take me out of my funk. It was the first time I experienced joy in a long time. My sons, Barbara (my daughter-in-law), Laura, my daughter, and her friend joined us for an exciting adventure.

While everyone went snorkeling and swimming, I took long walks on the beach. I just reflected on my life and what I wanted to do next. By decompressing in such a lovely place, I was able to write an article about how much hospice had helped our family. As I was writing, I saw doves land on the veranda. I felt connected to Paul and that something very special was happening.

Eventually, I submitted the article to my local paper, and they published it. Little did I know at the time that my feature article, "The Angel at the Door," would lead to opportunities for me to get outside of my own needs and open up a new chapter in my life. It led to my becoming more involved with hospice, and it enabled me to give back by sharing my story, learning, and helping others.

While that trip to Hawaii was a great break from my routine and an opportunity to reflect on what mattered, it's not always practical—from a time, logistics, or financial standpoint—to use travel as a tool for healing. However, you could achieve similar results by connecting with friends, family, or even new groups of people in an environment that gives you a break from your everyday life.

Visit someone you know in another city, or tour with a group, and use that time to meditate and reflect upon what's meaningful to you. Or plan to go to a local park, museum, or other place where you can relax. If you live near a beach, lake, river, pond, or other area surrounded by natural beauty, take advantage of it. (I'll discuss more about the healing power of travel in chapter 4.)

 Tip

If you're a person who must constantly check your smartphone, try turning it off during these decompression excursions. It's difficult to relax if you feel bombarded by texts, emails, or alerts. While cell phones and text messages are great for staying connected, they also may exacerbate anxiety when you are trying give yourself time to breathe and to be fully present to your surroundings. Sometimes it's helpful to disconnect for brief periods, even if it's just a few hours, especially when you're traveling and want some quiet time. If you haven't finished this book, consider bringing it along on a trip and reading it. Or take another book that appeals to you.

At some point, you may even visit a familiar vacation spot or local attraction with a potential future partner. I'll discuss new relationships in more detail later in this book, but I want you to be aware that you need to be prepared for those excursions.

About eleven years after Paul died, I went with Jack on a trip to Austin. I was leery because Paul and I had visited some of the same sites there just about a year before he was diagnosed with cancer. I didn't know what it would be like to visit Austin with a man other than Paul, but I had enjoyed the city so much that I was ready to give it a try.

My goal in Austin was to see some of the familiar places, such as the Lyndon Johnson Library and downtown Austin. I also wanted to enjoy new experiences in the city. When Jack and I got to the library, I realized that enough time had passed that I could be just as happy there with him as I had been with Paul. We stayed at a different hotel than on my last trip with Paul, ate at different restaurants, and experienced something new by going into a venue where they played jazz and other music. Although Jack and I were the oldest people in the room, we took over the dance floor. What a relief and joy it was to visit a familiar city with fresh eyes and really enjoy the trip!

To sum it up, you can go back to some of the old places where you once shared fond memories. Based on my own experience and what other people who've lost their spouses or partners have told me, be sure to proceed cautiously. Understand that you may feel a mix of sadness and joy, yet know that engaging in these adventures should get easier for you to do and will be more enjoyable as time goes on.

> To sum it up, you can go back to some of the old places where you once shared fond memories.

DEALING WITH MEMORIAL SERVICES, FUNERALS, AND THE NEED FOR CLOSURE

In many religions, the service for a loved one must happen within a very short period after his or her death. Some religions offer more flexibility regarding when a service should occur. Planning a service may seem overwhelming to the person who just lost a loved one, and it may be more convenient to wait a month or more. A significant delay, however, can cause people to get "stuck" and extend the denial phase of grief.

Based on my observations, I can understand why it's so critical to avoid delaying a service for more than a few weeks after someone dies. Some people I've known expressed a feeling of deep depression after a loss. They were barely able to get through the basic daily functions of life—eating, sleeping, and engaging in conversations with others.

Even months after their loved ones died, they still hadn't gotten around to having a service. Of course, they had a lot of excuses. It was too difficult to get the family together and coordinate everyone's schedules. Their work was too demanding. It would be better to wait for summer, when the weather was nicer, and so on. When they finally had a service, however, it seemed to help offer them closure. Plus, they generally became less anxious and more engaged with other people, the tasks ahead of them, and new activities.

Keep in mind that a service doesn't have to be a major event. It could be something as basic as getting a small group of family and friends together for a simple ceremony, particularly if this is a memorial service.

> When Karen's father died, for example, Karen's husband led a service in the senior home where her dad had lived. People gathered, shared stories about him, and celebrated with cake, coffee, and cookies. It was a modest and dignified service that was done in a timely manner, and it helped bring her family together. Another woman I know took her children on a boat ride to her late husband's favorite place, a local lake, where they said prayers and honored him.

If you've lost a loved one and haven't done a service, consider doing one soon. You may be surprised by how much the act of being surrounded by people to support you helps to give the closure necessary to move on.

Some religions have additional services a year after a person's death—experiencing another service a year later may be part of your tradition. You may find this comforting, or one service may be all you can handle. You'll determine which approach is best for you, based on your unique needs and your religious beliefs.

Working through grief is a complicated process. By journaling, releasing anger, getting help, forgiving yourself and others, and following some of the other suggestions I've discussed, you can help to ease the pain of grief.

CHAPTER 2

▼

Developing Strategies for Moving Forward

GAINING INSIGHT THROUGH LOSS AND FINDING OPPORTUNITIES FOR GROWTH

When Paul was ill, a hospice social worker said to me, "Hospice can be beautiful." I thought, *Are you crazy? My husband is dying. What can be beautiful about that?*

Many months after Paul passed away, I finally figured out what the social worker was trying to convey. Hospice care gave him the opportunity to be in his own home and get guidance from the hospice chaplain. It enabled me to play a role in keeping him calm during this difficult time. I discovered the depths of love that I never thought were imaginable. I read stories to him each night, some that I had written. We savored every moment when he was well enough to walk, talk, eat, and visit with friends and family. We cherished his good days and appreciated simple things, like being able to take a ride in the car to look at the outside scenery or to listen to music at home.

Paul told me about his dreams of pages on calendars breaking away, an indication that he was running out of time. By watching him die, I realized how important it was to focus on finding simple joys in life after his passing. I stopped complaining about petty issues related to people and politics. It was no longer worth it to sweat the small stuff or become annoyed when I got stuck in traffic. I became a calmer and more patient person. I remembered to slow myself down, and I took the time to thank people for their kindness, whether it was my friends, coworkers, or the clerk at the grocery store who packaged my items.

The loss was tragic, but it helped to make me a better person. I was grateful to be alive. I would tell people who complained relentlessly about their work to take a step back and be happy that they had a job and were healthy. I advised my friends that if they had concerns about their work, they should talk to their managers and try to resolve any issues, instead of complaining. If those problems weren't solvable, then I explained how they should consider a plan to either accept what they couldn't change or pursue another opportunity.

Basically, I thought these people needed to put the issues related to work into perspective. You may be able to control certain aspects of what you do with your job. When you lose a loved one, though, everything changes in your life. Fretting over a promotion you didn't get or feeling slighted when you're not recognized for a job well done seems less important than dealing with life and death issues.

All of my life, I have had an intense focus on my career, often to the detriment of so many other important personal priorities. While I tended to spend too much time working, at the cost of having a more balanced life, watching Paul die made me focus on my values. What good is money when your loved one is gone? I realized that placing too much emphasis on financial objectives and the need to satisfy my ego was much less significant than my quest for improving my health and well-being and achieving a more balanced and meaningful life.

GETTING THE SUPPORT OF YOUR FAMILY AND FRIENDS

I'm not saying that you can change who you are overnight just because you've suffered a loss, but it's safe to assume that you'll look at the concept of time very differently when you come face-to-face with the reality that time is limited.

Where can this new insight lead you? Some people begin to reassess their priorities. For example, if spending more time with your children, grandchildren, parents, or friends is important, then develop a plan to make that happen.

It was important for me to make spending time with my adult children, growing number of grandchildren, and other family members a priority. For example, Kevin's family lives within a reasonable driving distance, and it has been wonderful watching the grandkids grow up. My son Michael, daughter-in-law Kali, and their children were a short flight away for many years, but I've tried to visit with them as often as I can. I often travel a distance to visit with my mom, Laura (my daughter), Megan (my stepdaughter), and many other relatives. It's well worth the effort to stay connected.

Your calendar—whether it's on your phone, wall, or in a planner— can become a trusted assistant. Schedule time to be with people you enjoy. If you were a caretaker, chances are that you put many of your own priorities on hold. Now it's time to take care of yourself.

Contact the people you want to be with and arrange to see them. For example, if you have adult children who live nearby, see if you can schedule a weekly or biweekly dinner or lunch. If you have grandchildren, volunteer to babysit when you can and give their parents a night out. It's amazing how healing it can be to get to know your grandkids better, and they can benefit from the attention too. I cherish the moments with my grandchildren, and watching them grow up brings me so much joy.

The same approach to planning applies to spending time with your friends. Schedule activities with them. Contact the people who are important to you and see when they might be available to meet. It will give you something to look forward to each week.

You may have friends who also find themselves alone after being in a coupled relationship. They might appreciate the opportunity to have a companion to join them for a meal, go to a movie or play, or even take a trip.

One woman I know gets together with another widow in her neighborhood once a week. They go to each other's homes and watch movies and then discuss the plots over coffee. Your activities don't have to cost anything. You just need to find a way to connect with others. It's worth the effort.

Many research reports indicate that people who are lonely are much more likely to have shorter lives than those who are actively engaged with others. In fact, some leading studies have concluded that loneliness is a greater health-risk factor than obesity and that social isolation can increase your mortality risk dramatically.

If you are in a situation where you don't see friends and family very often, then consider joining a group of people who share your common interests. Visit Meetup.org, and sign up for an activity that appeals to you, or go to your local community center to find out about activities in your area, such as day trips, workshops, classes, exercise programs, and volunteer work.

REDISCOVERING YOURSELF

Loss gives you the opportunity to reflect on who you are and what you want to do with the rest of your life.

One widow, Li Na, had been her husband's caretaker for many years. During that time, she stopped working as a teacher, cut back on social engagements, and put all of her energies into keeping her husband safe and comfortable. After he had died, Li Na, who was about seventy, realized that she always wanted to be an artist. She had never pursued that interest because she had been too busy earning a living as a teacher.

After her husband passed away, Li Na enrolled in community college art classes and hired an art tutor. Her watercolor paintings blossomed into masterpieces that were on display in local galleries, museums, and stores. She discovered that creative expression was her ticket to happiness. Today, she's very involved in the arts and participates in gatherings with other artists. Whenever I see her, she's always smiling. The artist within her emerged, and she found a talent that she never knew existed. Creating art became her new love and passion.

EMBRACING THE POWER OF MAKING A DIFFERENCE

One way to soothe grief is to get outside of yourself and assist other people. That's where volunteering for an organization that you believe in can help you as much as it helps others. There are so many ways you can make a difference when you're ready. Here's an example:

> One retired widower, George, found joy in tutoring science courses to underprivileged students. He was devastated when his wife of forty years died. About a year later, he began the tutoring sessions, which were so much more rewarding to him than his demanding corporate job. The students really appreciated the individual attention and expertise that he provided. George also found great happiness in spending time with his children and grandchildren.
>
> Leslie ran a printing business with her partner, Wendy, which she closed after Wendy died. Leslie wanted to find something additional to occupy her time, help people in her community, and give her a reason to leave the house each day. About six months after Wendy's sudden death, Leslie volunteered at a local organization that provided clothing, household items, furniture, and other resources to those in need. Leslie said that the volunteer work gave her life structure, which she was missing, as well as a chance to make a difference. She also enjoyed the social contact with other volunteers and made some new friends through this organization.

Hector worked in the fast-paced, high-tech world as a chief technology officer, but he revaluated his life after his wife died of cancer. The sixty-hours workweeks were taking a toll on his health and his ability to enjoy the limited spare time he had available. He switched careers, took a pay cut, and got a job with a forty-hour workweek for a nonprofit that provided medical services to people in need. Reducing his workload left him with more time to exercise on a regular basis to improve his health. Hector was proud of his new career, and he developed friendships with people at work who share his common interests and goals.

Whatever insight you glean from your loss can shape your volunteer work, career, relationships, health, and goals. You can't make the loss go away, but you can use it to help you transform and grow.

CHAPTER 3

▼

TAKING CONTROL

DEFINING WHO YOU ARE NOW AND WHAT YOU WANT

Losing a spouse or partner is very different from other losses. Your other half is generally with you on a daily basis. When this person dies, your identity as a couple suddenly fades. Now it's just you. This obvious revelation didn't fully sink in for me until I filled out an application for an account and had to check "single" in the box instead of married. I thought, *How did this happen? I didn't ask to become single. I'm not ready to move into this category. Now what am I going to do?*

As difficult as it was to admit that I couldn't return to my old life, I truly empathized with many of the people a generation older than me who experienced a similar loss. Here's an example:

> Grace lived in a home in the woods in California. She was married for sixty-five years to her high school sweetheart, and her daughter lived in Europe. She didn't have any siblings or cousins. Her husband paid all the bills, and Grace tended to the garden and household. Because her home was in a remote location, she didn't have neighbors nearby to check

in on her. Most of her longtime friends who were still alive had moved out of state. It was a twenty-minute drive into her local town. Her eyes weren't as sharp as in the past, and she stopped driving at age eighty-five.

Grace finally realized that she needed some assistance after her husband died but wasn't sure how to make that happen. While it's generally a good idea not to make major changes, like moving and quitting your job, until at least a year after a loss, Grace's circumstances were an exception. She couldn't afford to maintain the home on her own, and she was living in a place where her closest neighbors were about a quarter-mile away. A friend suggested that Grace look into selling her home and moving to a community where she'd have a support system and would be more centrally located.

Relocating was the first major decision that Grace made on her own without her husband. She knew it wasn't going to be easy to leave her house of many years, the home she loved. Leaving this home felt like another loss, but she believed it was the right decision. Besides, she was so lonely living in a remote environment without her husband.

With the help of a financial planner and realtor, Grace decided to sell the house and move into a retirement community. At first, it was very difficult to leave her home and its memories and to part with many of the furnishings and items that simply would not fit in her tiny residential unit. She knew, however, that it was impractical to remain in her home.

Gradually, Grace became used to the new environment and enjoyed socializing with many of the residents. She found it empowering to make her own decisions about where to live, what movie to see, and what restaurant to visit and to be unencumbered with the responsibility of maintaining a house. She learned how to pay the bills and take over responsibilities that her husband had always handled.

Ultimately, she transformed from a quiet, introverted wife, living in the country, to an outgoing woman who enjoyed socializing, visiting local museums and shops, and becoming involved in her community activities. Being on her own taught her that even though she missed her husband, she was capable of being self-sufficient and happy.

Here's another example of someone who was able to make a positive change in his life after the loss of his wife:

Henry, who owned a computer-repair shop with his wife, Vicky, always wanted to return to college and get a computer science degree, but he kept putting it off due to his ongoing personal responsibilities. He worked long days to pay for their house. As his family grew, it became less likely that he'd ever have the time to attend college. There was always something that took priority over his getting a degree.

About a year after his wife died, Henry, who was forty-six at the time, decided to pursue his dream of a college degree. His kids had moved out of the house and had gone off to college. He was lonely, but for the first time in many years, he finally had enough flexibility to return to school.

Henry cut his work back to thirty hours a week and hired someone to help manage his repair business so that he could attend classes. While losing Vicky was devastating, Henry knew he couldn't do anything to change that situation. Since his personal obligations were no longer holding him back, and he could afford to hire an assistant, he pursued his long-term goal of being a software developer. A few years after Henry returned to college, he got a degree in computer science.

Henry eventually sold his repair business. Today, he enjoys the team environment of working at a high-tech startup and the challenge of developing software. The new company he works for has a baseball team that meets on weekends, and he was excited to join the team. Henry likes the camaraderie of this working environment and the opportunity to develop friendships for his new life.

Anita is another example of how to find an opportunity after a loss:

Anita moved to Los Angeles to be with her partner, Dan, but never really liked the city and the traffic. When her kids were growing up, Anita worked full time as a realtor and regretted not being able to attend their soccer games or school programs.

After Dan died, following a long illness, Anita eventually moved to Phoenix, Arizona, to be near her children, grandchildren, elderly parents, and siblings. It made sense financially because the cost of living was considerably less in Phoenix than in Los Angeles. Anita knew she'd miss her friends from Los Angeles and that starting over in a new community in her sixties and building a new network of friends wouldn't be easy. To avoid rushing into making a big change, she waited more than a year after Dan died before she moved.

Relocating to Phoenix was just what she needed to rebuild her life. Anita enjoyed babysitting her grandchildren two days a week and working part-time in a bookstore. The job paid considerably less than what she had earned as a realtor in Los Angeles, but that no longer mattered to her.

The part-time job provided some income to supplement her retirement, and it freed up her time to cultivate a social network as she established herself in this new community. Babysitting the grandkids gave Anita the opportunity to experience some of what she had missed when her own children were growing up. Having her family nearby provided comfort as she dealt with the loss of her husband and began assimilating into a new environment.

Starting over after a loss is a big adjustment, but these people were able to define goals and build new memories to give meaning and happiness to their lives. It may take you months, or even a year or more, to think about how to reshape the direction of your life, whether it involves moving, changing careers, adopting new habits, finding new friends, or volunteering. Take your time, and set manageable expectations. Move at a pace that's comfortable.

Don't try to take on more than you can handle, or you'll get so caught up in day-to-day tasks that it will be difficult to focus strategically on what you need to do to meet your long-term goals.

For the first six months or so after a loss, you may feel like you're about half as productive as in the past. That's to be expected because you're still absorbing the loss and adjusting to its impact. If you used to accomplish four major errands in a day, it may be a stretch to do more than two. If you used to enjoy cooking meals, you may feel that cooking is too much effort, so you buy food that you simply warm up in a microwave. It may take you twice as long to catch up on your paperwork, such as paying bills, organizing appointments, and so on. That's okay. You're still grieving, so set reasonable goals and expectations.

Try to plan activities for each week in advance. It's helpful to build more structure into your schedule, such as taking an exercise class or attending a community event a few days a week. Be sure to also allow yourself enough time to decompress from your loss.

Don't underestimate the extra work you have to do now that your partner or spouse isn't there to help. You may have shared chores, and now you need to carry a double load with new responsibilities. This could include having to develop skills related to bill paying, accounting, cooking, tending to a garden, or fixing broken appliances. The list goes on and on. Go easy on yourself, and get help from a friend or expert, when needed. In my case, I tracked down a handyman to take over a lot of the household repairs that came intuitively to Paul but that were difficult or seemed impossible for me to do.

You can do certain things to help cope with the extra burden you face when you lose your loved one. Set boundaries with others, based on how much time you can comfortably interact with people, and prioritize your personal goals and social objectives.

- If your annual visit to see Aunt Della in another city is expensive, emotionally draining, logistically difficult, and time-consuming, tell her you simply can't make it this year, but you'll keep in touch by phone or email.
- If you used to cook family dinners for the holidays, and it's just too much effort, consider having someone else do that instead.
- If your sister wants to visit from out of town and stay with you for two weeks, and you don't feel like company, then just say no. Explain that you're not ready for guests.

Give yourself permission to do what you need to do to feel better. If that means creating space for self-discovery and grieving, so be it.

DECLUTTERING: ADDRESSING PHYSICAL AND EMOTIONAL CHALLENGES

I've known people who have lost their spouses decades ago, yet their homes have never changed. Keeping everything the same can be comforting for a while. Ultimately, however, that can make it more difficult for some people to move forward with their lives.

Lena was forty when her husband died from cancer. For the first ten years following his death, she stayed in the same house and didn't make any changes to it. Her late husband's clothes remained in the closet she had shared with him and in the dressers in her bedroom. His pictures covered the walls, and his office remained untouched. The house was frozen in time, and Lena was lonely. Yet in those ten years, Lena never dated and rarely socialized, except for attending her children's school events. She just managed to get through each day and rarely experienced joy.

By the time Lena's kids went off to college, she decided it was time to begin socializing, even though she wasn't interested in having another relationship. When she finally met a man who had all of the traits that appealed to her, Lena discovered that she was ready to engage in a social life again. But before that could happen, she thought it was important to make some changes in her environment to reflect where she was at the present, instead of living in the past.

Lena was finally able to declutter her home. She still kept pictures of her husband on the walls, but they were mainly in her spare bedroom, hallway, and office, instead of everywhere throughout the house. She redecorated the master bedroom with new accessories and gave away her husband's clothes and his items that were in the room. She turned his office into a guest room, put some of his treasured items in a box, and donated many of his other belongings to charity.

Some people declutter their household immediately after the death; others do so over time. Move at the pace that's most comfortable to you. You can find special ways and places in your home to preserve certain memories of your loved one, while still making enough changes to accommodate your new situation. Here are some steps that can help you get started:

Decluttering Action Plan

- As soon as you feel comfortable, consider emptying the master bedroom closets and drawers of your loved one's stuff. You don't have to get rid of these things right away, and you might want to keep certain items for sentimental value. For many people, though, it's too painful to look at clothes in a closet, knowing that their loved ones are not coming back.
- Store these and other personal items in a place where you won't have to see them on a daily basis. Consider moving them temporarily to a garage, if you have one. When you're emotionally ready, you can determine what you want to donate, give away to friends or relatives, keep, or sell. Also, you can always take pictures of certain sentimental items and put them in a scrapbook.
- If your partner or spouse had an office in the house, the same guideline applies. Sort through the items that you want, and then move, donate, or get rid of everything else.
- Think about changes in your environment that might give you a fresh start. Paul, for example, died in a hospital bed in our bedroom. I had trouble sleeping at night until I was able to change the look of the room. I didn't want to go to the

expense of buying new furniture at the time, but I got new sheets, blankets, accessories, and a bedspread. I even painted the walls a different color.

My friends took Paul's clothes out of the closet we shared shortly after he died, and they put them in the garage for me to deal with when I was ready. Not everyone feels comfortable making that change so soon, but it worked for me. I also bought new towels and accessories for the master bathroom.

I still kept some pictures of Paul on walls in the house, but eventually I moved them out of the bedroom. Some people might find it more comfortable to be surrounded by those pictures everywhere. I didn't.

- Get a big storage box or chest, and keep it as a memory box. I got a five-by-three-foot chest and filled it with cards and letters that Paul had given me, pictures, various memorabilia, videos, his journals, and other items I wanted to save. I kept this big memory box in a closet and knew that whenever I needed to connect with Paul, I had one place in my home where I could go to think about him. This was really helpful, and visiting the memory box became a routine for me on his birthday, our wedding anniversary, the date of his passing, and other times.

Having this special place made it easier to transition to my new life because I could "visit with him" when I needed that connection. I was also able to focus more on living in the present because this box was in one central location. Although I chose to make a memory box, you might prefer creating an altar in your home or garden or some other option.

DECIDING IF YOU SHOULD RELOCATE

Moving to a new place provides an incentive for decluttering your life. As I mentioned earlier, it's generally not advisable to make life-changing decisions, like moving, until at least one year after your loss. That's because most people are so overwhelmed with the impact of losing their loved one that another big change, even if it's positive, just adds an additional stress to their lives.

If you have children still at home, any move can be disruptive because the kids already have to get used to living without Mom or Dad. Moving creates another adjustment that they may not be prepared to deal with at the time. You and your friends may have a social network in your community, and that network can be an ongoing source of support, structure, and normalcy.

In my case, I had always intended to leave the suburbs and move to the beach after Laura went off to college. Many of my friends and their families lived in my suburban neighborhood, but I was the only single person in our close-knit group. I stayed there for six years after Paul's death because it made more sense financially, and Laura had a familiar place to return to when she came home to visit me.

The real estate market dropped in late 2012, and I was able to downsize to a small townhome. I looked at a lot of properties before making my decision and walked around the new area frequently to get a feel for the neighborhood. I even talked to my prospective neighbors to see who lived in that community and why they liked living there to determine how I would fit in. I wanted to create new memories in a different place. Fortunately, the new development ultimately provided the same type of friendly community as the one I had left.

Some people move soon after a loss, and it's not always because they wanted to leave. Sometimes it's a matter of survival. Many senior citizens I've known have had to travel great distances from their homes after losing their spouses or partners. They relocated, out of necessity, to be near their adult children and grandchildren. While this provided a great opportunity for them to be close to family, they often made significant sacrifices. They gave up being close to longtime friends and having a home, rather than living in a smaller apartment, home, or a room in a senior residential development. Some had to sell precious items in order to pay for living expenses.

When they made new friends in these senior residences, they dealt with the emotional reality that the friends they had lunch with one day might be gone—pass away—the next. That happens more often when you reach your eighties, nineties, and beyond. Other seniors had to cope with the adjustment of moving in with their children after so many years of being independent.

Before you move from your current residence for economic, health, or family-related issues, ask the following questions:

1. What is the financial impact of this decision?
2. Assuming that you are considering moving only because you can't afford to live in your current place on your own, have you thought about renting out a room in your home for extra income? Although this option isn't for everyone, you might like it because it provides income, and you might enjoy having the company of a roommate.
3. What are the advantages of moving to be near family, compared with the disadvantages of giving up proximity to your friends and social network?
4. Assuming that you're still working, what impact will this have on your career?
5. When you get older, will you have physical problems that make it difficult to live in a two-story home, rather than a one-story residence? Although this might not apply to you now, I know many people who had to sell their two-story homes as they got older because of the difficulty of going up and down the stairs.
6. Do you need a security system to feel safe in your new neighborhood?
7. Are there people nearby who can help you in an emergency?

8. Are you close enough to services, shopping, transportation, medical care, and places with social activities? (If you move from a city where you led an active life to a remote location to be with your family, will you feel too isolated?)

9. Can you handle the upkeep of your current residence? For example, you may want to consider downsizing to a place with a smaller yard or a townhome or condo to limit the amount of yardwork and maintenance.

10. Are you moving toward something or running away from something? If the answer is the latter, what are you running away from?

Once you've made your decision to move, even if it's the best choice and you know that you will ultimately be very happy in your new residence, you may still miss the place you left behind. It takes time to adjust to change, and the decision to move is a big change that shouldn't be done impulsively. However, if you made a strategic choice based on your situation, goals, and values, you could discover that you're happier in your new environment.

REACHING OUT TO AVOID LONELINESS, EVEN WHEN YOU'RE AFRAID

Remember how easy it was to meet others when you were a child? You showed up at school, activities were planned, and you sat with many kids in the cafeteria. Perhaps you got involved in sports or Scouts. There were always people around and group activities to keep you busy.

Your situation today could be much different. You may be retired, living in an isolated area, or have a job that saps too much of your energy and time. You might need to provide extensive care for your children or parents. Perhaps you must deal with your own health limitations that make it more difficult to branch out and establish new friendships and engage in new experiences. Fortunately, there are things you can do to stay active and socially involved to help avoid the pitfalls of loneliness.

Set Personal Goals

If your objective is to meet a few new, good friends a year, then make that one of your goals, and develop a strategy for meeting people.

- **Become involved in activities that interest you.** If you like to read books, for example, contact your local bookstore, and find out if there are openings at a book club in your community. Or go online and search the name of your city and book clubs to see if there is one that you can join. I recently joined a book club that one of my friends started. We meet once a month, and I found it an excellent way to make new friends. Plus, I enjoy reading new books.

- **Join organizations.** Another way to become engaged in activities and meet people with similar interests is through Meetup.org. A friend of mine who was a widow enjoyed cycling but didn't want to ride alone. She went to the Meetup website and joined a local cycling club. It gave her the opportunity to become friends with new people and to exercise—a true win/win. There are meetups for just about any type of interest— art, music, hiking, writing, woodworking, fishing, and so on.

- **Cultivate a hobby.** Having a hobby can lead to new friendships, as in this example:

   Tim enjoyed acting in plays when he was in college thirty years ago. When his partner, Jason, died, Tim settled into a rut of eating fast food and spending too much time at night on the computer or watching TV. Tim's relatives lived out of state, so even though family outings provided Tim with comfort, they only occurred a few times a year.

A friend of Tim's encouraged him to take up a hobby. That's when he decided to join his local community theater group. Soon, he began appearing in local performances. Acting gave Tim a sense of fulfillment and provided more structure to his life. The more he became involved in acting, the more his everyday routines became increasingly stable. His eating habits got better, and he met new friends.

- **Take a class.** If you want to explore special classes, even if you have a college degree, consider enrolling in your local community college or attending individual workshops sponsored by your city. If you're a senior citizen, think about taking lifelong learning courses at your local college or within your community. They can provide an opportunity to learn about topics of interest to you, whether it's a foreign language, history, cooking, literature, science, or other topics. Some of the people who attend these classes may also become part of your social network.

Seniors may have more physical limitations that interfere with socializing, but many of these challenges can be overcome. For example, if health issues prevent you from driving, then transportation services, like Lyft and Uber, can take you to events. As you get older, it may be more difficult to drive at night. Instead of staying at home, think about alternate transportation options.

Many communities have senior centers that offer exercise classes, luncheons, interesting speakers, workshops, and trips to local movies and events. I encourage the seniors in grief groups to visit these centers, which offer a social network that can provide comfort and companionship. There are also many interesting activities that cover a wide range of interests.

When my stepfather died, we had his memorial service at a senior center where he had attended classes, led hikes, and developed friendships. I got to meet many of those people at his service, and they offered much-appreciated support to my mother. At eighty-eight, she's an active member of her local center and attends events with the friends she has met there.

Many of the people who've participated in grief-support workshops have also found comfort in going to their churches, temples, and other religious and spiritual organizations. These places also offer a variety of social activities, such as dinners, classes, and volunteer programs. All of these activities can provide additional structure, companionship, and support.

HEALING THROUGH VOLUNTEERING, WORKING, AND LOVING YOUR PET

As I discussed earlier, volunteer work offers an excellent opportunity to meet people and make a difference. If you enjoy working with children, consider volunteering at a local school or place of worship. There are mentoring programs, like the Boy's and Girl's Clubs, Big Brother/Sister programs, and career coaching. You might be interested in delivering Meals on Wheels to people who can't leave their homes. Or contact FeedingAmerica.org to find your local food bank, and donate your time.

Do you have a special skill, like playing the piano, cooking, singing, creating arts and crafts, writing, developing business plans, or another expertise? Look into volunteer opportunities that leverage your skills. Visit Volunteermatch.org to learn more about volunteer opportunities in your community. Various communities have programs to help clean up the environment, make calls from your home to support causes that you believe in, serve as a veterans' benefits coach, play music for hospice patients, work with animals, and more.

If you are actively employed and work in a physical office with others (as opposed to being a telecommuter), you have the advantage of a built-in network that can provide continuity and stability. Yes, it may be difficult to go to work each day when you are dealing with loss, but if your work is something that you enjoy, and you are in a supportive environment, then consider yourself fortunate. Working in a familiar environment can provide a sense of normalcy in your life. While you also need to process your grief, working with others can be enjoyable and give you a sense of accomplishment.

Don't underestimate the advantage of having a pet. It's comforting to know that when you open the door to your home, your place will feel less lonely because your dog will greet you with unconditional love. Dogs are family members too, and when you're the only remaining human at home, your dog can encourage you to get outside, walk, and enjoy the fresh air. Although I'm not much of a cat person, I've known some cats that give the same type of affection as friendly dogs. Cats also require much less maintenance.

I'm not advocating that you get a dog immediately because they are a big responsibility, but if you already have one, consider taking it to a dog park. That's another place where people congregate. It gives you the opportunity to exercise and get to know some of your neighbors.

TACKLING MONEY ISSUES AND FAMILY DYNAMICS

Reaching out also entails dealing with complex and often difficult topics, such as making financial decisions and working through what can be emotionally charged family expectations. Let's explore some of these challenges.

Your financial situation may become very different when you lose a spouse or partner, and it can impact the actions you take. It's not uncommon to go through a huge portion of your savings to take care of your loved one. If your spouse or partner was previously the key breadwinner for the household, those earnings may have dissipated after a lingering illness because that person could no longer work.

Medical bills, outside care, and insurance can be extremely costly. If your spouse or partner had a long career ahead, there's a remaining lifetime of lost income that you had expected.

To make matters worse, if you've been out of the workforce for a long time or aren't in a position to work, your lifestyle may have to change dramatically in ways you hadn't imagined. That's why it's so important to address these types of issues and to have a plan to deal with them. Here are some examples:

> Lisa's husband, Al, committed suicide, and Lisa had to deal with the emotional and financial impact of his death. Al had a debilitating but not life-threating illness and was being treated for depression before he died. When a partner or spouse commits suicide, the loss can be even greater because the survivor may go through the trauma of thinking there was something that he or she could have done to have prevented the suicide. People may blame themselves for things that were not their fault or under their control. Lisa went through extensive therapy to deal with this tragic loss. Six months later, she also joined a grief group.
>
> With the help of a friend who was also a financial adviser, Lisa looked at her options. Because the death was a suicide, she wasn't entitled to life insurance. She had gone through most of their savings during his illness and realized that she couldn't afford the full monthly payment of her home on her current salary. She was in no position, emotionally or physically, to take on the responsibility of finding a second job or looking for another one with a higher salary. She needed an extra six hundred dollars a month to stay in her same home and maintain her existing lifestyle.
>
> The adviser gave her a suggestion: rent out the downstairs bedroom. Having a roommate wasn't anything that Lisa had originally considered, but

eventually, she decided to do this because she wasn't ready to sell her house, move, or look for another job.

After screening numerous applicants, she selected Sally. As it turned out, she and Sally became friends. Sally helped Lisa cope with her loss. Lisa enjoyed having company, and Sally lived there for many years before Lisa got a new job, sold the house at a nice profit, and downsized.

Loss creates circumstances for which you likely are not prepared, but if you keep an open mind, you can work through them. Here's another example:

Dean, who relied on his Social Security checks as his main source of support, lived in a one-bedroom apartment with his partner, Jake. After Jake passed away from cancer, Dean was concerned because the mounting costs for home health-care workers, which weren't covered by Medicare, had eaten away at his savings. He had no financial flexibility to pay anything beyond routine bills. Dean was a retired carpenter who was eighty years old. His options for making a living were extremely limited.

Dean moved in with his nephew's family. It was an adjustment to make that change. Dean was determined to do whatever he could to repay his nephew, Ernie, for his generosity. Although Dean was still grieving the loss of his partner, he discovered that being surrounded by family gave him something to look forward to each day. He walked the kids to school, did repairs on Ernie's house, and babysat for the family. It wasn't the life he'd planned, but Dean made it work.

Here's another situation where life got very complicated for the surviving partner:

> When Ellen's partner, Irv, passed away of a sudden heart attack, Irv's adult children inherited the house where Ellen and Irv had lived. They told Ellen that she had four months to either leave or purchase the house from them. Irv's children needed to sell it quickly because they couldn't afford the mortgage and costs of maintaining the place. Ellen didn't have the money to buy the house from them. Irv and Ellen were together for four years, but Irv never got around to setting up a life estate for Ellen.
>
> Ellen had left a great job in England five years earlier to move to San Francisco and join Irv. Although Ellen had some savings and a satisfactory job in San Francisco, she wasn't in a position to buy the house. She loved living in San Francisco and looked at other options, such as renting an apartment, but the cost of living there was well beyond what she could afford.
>
> Ultimately, Ellen decided to move back to England, where she could be close to her siblings, parents, and longtime friends. Eventually, she got a new job in England, but she had to cope with losing Irv and leaving a city she loved.

Here's another situation that's common and very complicated:

> When Susan and Larry got married, it was the second marriage for both of them. Larry and Susan each had two adult children from prior marriages. Susan was a widow, and Larry had been divorced for more than ten years. Larry moved into Susan's home, and they combined assets and created a trust and will. When Larry passed away, the entire estate

went to Susan, who updated her will, based on the plans she had made with Larry. The will gave half of the estate to Larry's children and the other half to Susan's children, upon Susan's death.

Larry's adult children didn't want to wait to receive money from their estate. They had economic and career challenges and felt that the money should be given to them now, when they needed it the most. Conversely, Susan's adult children felt that if Larry's "kids" were going to get an advance, then they should get an advance on the inheritance at the same time.

This whole situation was very upsetting to Susan, who was trying to cope with the stress of losing her husband. It seemed like the adult children were too focused on money. Besides, Susan was approaching eighty. She was concerned that if she gave away too many assets in advance that there wouldn't be enough for her if she ever needed 24/7 health care.

These were all legitimate concerns. Ultimately, Susan decided to keep peace in the family and to help those who truly needed it. She was willing to give each adult child on both sides of the family the same amount in advance each year, rather than giving to some now and not others. Of course, if any family member wanted to delay an advance, that was fine too. Susan was also very careful to limit the amount of the distributions to ensure that she could live the rest of her life without worrying that she'd run out of money to support her lifestyle.

Susan realized that her children and stepchildren were also grieving the loss of Larry. She continued keeping up the family traditions after Larry's death, such as getting everyone together for gatherings at certain times of the year. She kept in close contact with all of them. Susan tried to think about what

Larry would have done to maintain harmony in the family and how he would have dealt with any pressing issues and ensured that everyone was treated fairly.

When you're the survivor, you may need to look at updating your will and trust or creating one. An attorney who specializes in estate planning can help you.

If you and your husband were each other's executor and trustee, pay special attention to who you name as the successor in those roles when you die and who should have the power of attorney for financial matters and health care decisions. When there are many children and stepchildren involved, the decisions you make could mean the difference between having everyone get along and creating family feuds.

It's a good idea to discuss the details of your intentions for your will and trust with your children and stepchildren, consider their feedback, and ask your attorney for recommendations. If any of your potential heirs don't get along or if you have concerns about putting certain family members in these roles, you might consider having an independent third party handle these functions. You obviously need to look at the costs and get recommendations if the independent party isn't someone you know.

Some people are uncomfortable with discussing the status of their estate with family members. As a lone survivor, discussing what happens after you pass away may be a difficult topic to bring up with heirs. There's sometimes a fear that family members will start to make judgments or negative comments regarding how you spend your money. There's also the fear of losing control over your assets or having someone else make decisions about the care you'll receive if, in the future, you are not able to make these decisions for yourself.

However, failure to be transparent with your heirs, regardless of your concerns, can cause family conflicts that you may not have imagined. You may be concerned, for example, that your daughter, Julie, has economic needs that your son, Luke, doesn't have, and you want to leave a significantly greater portion of your estate to Julie. Or maybe one child has been very supportive and helpful, and the other has had a more distant relationship with you.

If you avoid discussing these issues, your family members won't have the opportunity to ask questions about their inheritance or your health care desires in advance. That approach can create lingering hurt feelings and conflict between your survivors.

> If you meet with Julie and Luke to discuss the reasons why you've made your decisions, at least you can get their input. Luke might tell you that he understands why you left more money to Julie. In fact, he may already be helping Julie because he's in a position to assist her. Without having this conversation, however, Luke might feel slighted and hurt. He might never realize what motivated your decision, other than his erroneous perception that you loved Julie more than you loved him.

People aren't mind-readers. Don't leave them guessing about why one sibling was treated one way, and the other was treated another.

An additional concern that causes some people to keep their financial details a secret is the worry that if family members know they will receive a potentially significant inheritance, they might spend money foolishly now and have an entitled mindset. It's a good idea to explain that you expect them to continue to be self-supporting, manage their finances effectively, and live within their means, regardless of what they might hope to inherit.

> If you had one adult child, Mia, who was distant from you for many years, and another daughter, Martha, who was very close, it's still a good idea to discuss in advance with both of them how they will be treated in your will and why you made this decision. You may discover that Mia was distant because she was coping with problems—health, career, depression,

a difficult marriage, or other issues—and her lack of communication was not related to you. She simply had to address her own problems before she could focus on being more responsive to your needs.

Mia may not have realized that her behavior upset you. Perhaps she lived several thousand miles away and had so many responsibilities that she didn't know that you were upset and wanted to spend more time with her. This insight into Mia's perspective may not impact how you deal with your estate, but a discussion about your concerns will give both of you more clarity. It may even bring the two of you closer together.

According to some industry research studies, the average lump-sum inheritance is gone within about five years due to financial mismanagement. That's why people need to be educated on how to manage an inheritance. Explain your values and expectations to your heirs.

What should you tell them? Let's look at your financial and health issues separately. For financial issues, gather information about your assets, liabilities, will, trust, plans, and intentions. Share what you are comfortable sharing with your family members, and give this and any other relevant information to your lawyer or trusted adviser. Let your beneficiaries know the people to contact for your accounts and policies. Remember that they will be grieving when you pass away. Do what you can now to make the process less painful for them.

Even if you don't want to go into detail about the state of your finances, at least find out if there's something that they would want so that family members don't fight over Dad's car, Mom's watch, who has to take care of your dog, and so on. They might want to know where to find a list of your friends to contact. If they inherit property, they'll need to know account information about loans, bills related to the property, life insurance policies, and so on.

It's emotionally draining and time-consuming to plan what happens after you pass away or become ill and need assistance, especially while you're grieving the loss of your loved one, but it's one of those tasks that needs to be addressed.

COMMUNICATING YOUR MEDICAL PRIORITIES

Now, let's look at how you expect your designees to deal with health care-related issues. If your spouse or partner was your designee on your advance-care directive for your health care, be sure to update that document with the names of the people you want to handle this for you. Discuss this responsibility with them first, to make sure they will accept it.

It's very important to complete an advance-care directive because when you need care, this document will help ensure that it's done according to your wishes. Your local hospice may have forms and educational sessions on completing this document. Estate-planning attorneys can also help. Fill out the forms, along with the phone numbers of people to contact in an emergency, and put these on your refrigerator or some place that is easily visible. Make sure that your designees also have information about your long-term health care policy, if you have one.

They should know the medications you take and the dosage, as well as the contact information for your doctors. If you have a neighbor or friend who checks in on you on a regular basis, share this information with your designees and neighbor or friend. Make sure they exchange phone numbers in case of an emergency.

There are times when family members turn against each other because they were disappointed in the way the estate was handled or because certain relatives were put in a position of trust but betrayed the wishes of the departed. If you're concerned about what will happen when you pass away, give these decisions a lot of thought. Consult with advisers you respect, family members, and even therapists, who might be able to provide more insight into this important matter.

DEALING WITH EMOTIONAL TRIGGERS

As you may have experienced, the first year following a loss is particularly difficult because you're bombarded with so many changes, and you're not sure how certain milestones (your anniversary, birthdays, holidays, etc.) or situations will impact you. If you're prepared, however, you can turn a potentially difficult situation into a memorable and positive experience. For example, the year Paul died, I became increasingly nervous as his birthday approached. How could I possibly face his birthday without him? Then the answer dawned on me—*I'll give him a party.*

Suddenly, I changed the dynamics of that day from one of dread to an event that I looked forward to attending. I invited the friends who had helped to cook our family meals while he was sick, did errands, visited, and provided emotional support to help me through his illness. I asked them to think about a humorous or interesting memory of Paul that they could share, and I brought a photo album of his pictures to the dinner. We ate his favorite food and toasted him, and the day turned into a wonderful celebration and an opportunity to thank many of the people who had been so helpful when I needed their support.

I've shared this experience, and people have told me that taking this perspective on an upcoming birthday was very helpful to them. Some of them decided to have small celebrations with a few members of their family to get through similar milestones. Others visited places that their loved ones enjoyed, such as the beach and hiking trails, and brought friends and family there.

Every year I've tried to do something to honor Paul's memory on his birthday. For example, he loved driving along Highway 9 in Santa Cruz through the redwoods. I've taken that drive, listened to the music he enjoyed, and stopped off at the redwood forest—his favorite place. More recently, I established one popular tradition. I eat his favorite food—pizza and an ice cream sundae. I've shared this memorial ritual with family members and some of his friends, and this has become an annual practice for many of us each year.

My new husband, Jack, who also loves pizza and ice cream, participates in this ritual. He understands that even though many years have passed since Paul's death, and I'm very happy in my new relationship, it's still important to keep Paul's memory alive in this way.

The first anniversary is likely to be the most difficult one, so I encourage you to think about it in advance, and consider spending that time with friends or family. If you prefer to be alone, be extra kind to yourself that day, and know that you will get through it.

A friend of mine lost her husband around the same time that Paul died. We decided to take our daughters out to dinner on one of those early anniversaries and tried to make the best of it. The waitress looked at us innocently and said, "Are you celebrating a birthday?" My friend, looked at her and said, "Not exactly. We're celebrating a death day." The waitress stared at us and looked horrified until we explained that this dinner was how we'd decided to honor our late husbands on that day.

I was surprised to discover that happy occasions can also trigger loss because your spouse or partner isn't there to share those moments with you. When Paul's son, Forest, got married to a very nice woman, many years after Paul died, I wasn't prepared for my reaction. I looked at all of the people at the reception and ran out of the room to a quiet place and just started to cry.

It was totally out of character for me to get that emotional so long after Paul was gone. I was sad because it seemed unfair that Paul wasn't alive to share in this joyful event. After composing myself, I rejoined the group and was able to take part in the remainder of the celebration. Sometimes you just don't know when something will trigger an emotion that you haven't expected. Understand that these emotions are a normal part of grief.

The experience at Forest's wedding made me realize that when Laura got married two years after his wedding, I would have to contain those emotions and focus on enjoying the moment. By then, I was in a wonderful relationship with Jack and had come to terms with the fact that Paul wouldn't be alive to see her get married to her loving husband, Ian. I distinctly remember when Laura was seventeen, shortly after Paul died, and she burst into tears, saying, "But who will walk me down the aisle when I get married someday?"

That problem was solved. I proudly and happily took over and escorted her down the aisle. The tears I experienced were those of joy, not of sadness, because I had already worked through that emotion at Forest's wedding.

Another trigger is attending a funeral or memorial service.

> Gloria's husband, Michael, died just a few months before her good friend's husband, Juan, passed away. Gloria was able to hold back the tears and give a powerful message at her own husband's service. I knew, however, that she was keeping a lot of emotions inside and was still working through the initial shock of Michael's death.
>
> I gave Gloria some advice to help her get through Juan's service, which was a ninety-minute drive from her home. I told Gloria to be prepared for reliving her own grief and dealing with emotions that she might not have been able to express during Michael's memorial service. I reminded her that attending Juan's service could be unsettling. I asked her to find out who was going from her area and to get a ride from them. Driving in New York is hectic enough, and combined with the prospect of an emotionally laden event, she could have put herself at risk.
>
> Gloria cried throughout Juan's service, giving herself permission to release the emotions she had suppressed at her own husband's memorial service.
>
> Gloria's situation is another example of knowing that certain milestones or events, like weddings and funerals, can trigger unexpected emotions. It's important to be present at these events, but also be

prepared. Understand that your reactions are normal, and think about a plan for how to deal with them.

I regretted that Paul had missed other major events, such as the birth of our grandchildren and attending the college graduation ceremonies for Laura and Megan. Paul would have been so proud of his daughters. Somehow, I was able to get through those memorable occasions without the outburst that sprung forth at Forest's wedding.

Here's a list to help you cope with milestones and situations that could set off the feelings of loss:

Checklist to Prepare for Emotionally Laden Milestones

- **Weddings and Graduations:** Focus on the joy of the day. Write down in advance what you can do if you are overcome with regret that your loved one can't experience these events. Perhaps write a letter to your loved one before you go, explaining why you are sad that he or she can't experience this event. It helps to get that emotion out of your thoughts and onto paper so that you can work it out in advance.

- **Funerals and Memorial Services:** If you're attending a funeral too soon after your loss, consider whether you are emotionally ready to be there. Determine if the benefits of attending outweigh the feelings of being uncomfortable. Many people find these events healing, and in Gloria's case, it helped her to work through the unprocessed grief of her husband.

- **Births and Other Happy Events:** Journaling can help. Write a letter to your loved one and explain how you felt when watching the birth of your grandchild or attending the child's sporting event, confirmation, baptism, Bar Mitzvah, or other ceremony. Describe how this child may have inherited a particular talent or trait from your loved one that helps keep this person's memory alive through the generations.

- **Day-to-Day Difficulties:** It's common to experience times when we wish our spouses or partners could be there to guide us through a career crisis; health issues; concerns about children, grandchildren, and other relationships; or give advice on things like buying a new car.

  Even if you don't journal on a regular basis or you stopped journaling years before, write your loved one a letter and ask what you should do. If you're not into writing, just ask yourself how he or she would help you solve this problem. If you're not sure, and you still need assistance, check in with someone who knew your spouse or partner well.

  One widower kept wondering why his stepchildren would call him frequently with questions about how to deal with basic situations he thought they should be able to resolve on their own. He was the person who had been closest to their mom. So instead of considering it annoying, he could have taken it as a compliment that they trusted him enough to ask for his advice.

- **Special Songs:** Nothing seems to bring back old memories more than familiar songs. You could be enjoying a pleasant drive in the car along a scenic route, and then suddenly, the song that was special for you and your sweetheart blasts on the radio. You might find it comforting to hear that music, but those songs can also make you cry. Stay with your emotions, and know that the music you shared can create a response that could catch you off guard. Over time, it could bring a smile to your face.

As you begin to take control and proactively address the challenges presented by the loss of your loved one, you can become more confident in your ability to move forward with your life and experience joy and fulfillment. The loss involves dealing with many different issues related to your living situation, finances, activities, memories, and relationships. Prioritize how you will manage these changes. Don't overextend yourself. Avoid making too many decisions too soon.

CHAPTER 4

▼

GETTING TO KNOW THE NEW YOU

PUTTING THE RING AWAY—OR MOVING IT—AND CONTEMPLATING DATING

Depending on where you are in your grief journey, your age, and your unique circumstances, at some point you may decide to take the plunge and see what it's like to date again. This can be particularly scary if you were married for many years, and the very thought of dating again is not something you ever considered. Your friends may try to set you up or encourage you to start socializing, while your adult children may either support you or be horrified by the prospect of Mom or Dad going out. Don't give in to anyone's pressure either way. Just move at your own pace and take it slowly.

Keep in mind that you may be fragile and vulnerable after losing a spouse or partner. If your spouse had a long illness, for example, your grief began when that illness started. You might be ready to get back into the social world faster than someone who lost a loved one quickly and unexpectedly. Either way, take your time, because if you rush into a new relationship prematurely, you may not even realize that you're still grieving.

Although many people have found successful matches using dating websites, a one-on-one meeting may be too overwhelming for some people. Another approach is what I call *practice socializing.*

If you're working, attend a social event or seminar for people in your field. Don't even think about dating at this point. Just see if you have enough courage to go to an event that appeals to you, such as a seminar or religious gathering, with a group of strangers and if you can be comfortable enough to converse with people there.

I worked in the technology industry and would sometimes attend seminars related to technology trends. After Paul died, I decided to join a local organization that sponsored dinner meetings featuring presentations by industry leaders. I wasn't looking to meet any potential men to date. I just wanted to get some experience in moving outside of my comfort zone and learning how to network. The seminars were useful in educating me about issues related to my job. They also helped to give me confidence in interacting with people I didn't know. Once I conquered that challenge, I was ready to move on to the next one—the precursor to dating.

I went online and did a search of events for singles in my area, based on events that appealed to me. Most of my friends were married, and it took a lot of courage for me to attend several of these events alone. I wasn't ready for finding dates via dating websites, so attending in-person activities was more appealing to me.

One event included a weekly brunch, where a group of people my age gathered. One man seemed interesting to me, and the women in the group vouched for him. They said he was friendly, kind, and trustworthy. Eventually, I felt comfortable enough to accept his invitation to take me to dinner.

When he kissed me good night after one of our dates, I thanked him profusely because I hadn't known if I would ever be able to kiss anyone again after losing Paul. To my surprise and delight, I discovered I could. He was a very nice man, but I regret that I rushed into a relationship with him too soon after my loss. I thought I was ready for a companion. I wasn't. The relationship ended, but we parted as friends.

If meeting someone new is important to you, take your time, and when you're ready, give yourself permission to experience being with another person. Even though your loved one is no longer alive, try to release the feeling that you're somehow being unfaithful to your deceased spouse or partner. This may be difficult. If it's too much of a struggle for you, then you're probably not ready to start dating.

Another challenge is that you may not want to get too close to someone because you're afraid of experiencing loss again. Unfortunately, I've seen people sabotage their happiness by staying in less-than-satisfying relationships, simply because they didn't know whether they wanted it to last—the idea being that if the relationship is just so-so, then it won't hurt so much when it's over. To avoid this situation, take baby steps when you consider dating. Give yourself time to heal first.

> One engaging man in his eighties, Tony, who had been married for sixty years before his wife passed away, said he was ready to start meeting women. He asked me for some advice. He wanted companionship but not a relationship. I suggested that he attend luncheons at his local senior center and to talk to some of the women who were there.
>
> A week later, Tony told me that the women he met were friendly, but after five minutes or so, their conversations would end abruptly. I told Tony to take off his wedding ring or move it over his middle finger the next time he visited the senior center. I explained that these women thought he was still married, which is why they kept their conversations brief. Sure enough, after following my advice, Tony got a completely different reaction and said that he had great conversations with several women. He began dating one of them.

If you're ready to venture out and try meeting someone, you can still wear your wedding ring. Just move it to a place that says you're not married.

Sometimes when you're not looking for a relationship, it finds you. That was the case with Jack, who is now my husband. I was on the mend from my own medical scare in 2015 and decided it was time to get closer to God. I went to a gathering at my friend's house to learn about becoming a member of my local place of worship. This love story sounds like something that only happens in the movies, but in my case, while I was looking for God, I came across Jack, who also attended that event.

I wasn't ready to date when I first met him. Eventually, we got together, and I discovered how happy we made each other. We laughed at each other's jokes, enjoyed the same activities, and our families melded easily. I felt I was finally able to get my life back. In 2006, when Paul died, I never imagined that I could have such a loving and fulfilling life again, yet it happened. I don't ever take it for granted.

MEETING PEOPLE ONLINE

While my meeting Jack was truly serendipitous, you might prefer using an online dating resource, which I mentioned earlier. This gives you the opportunity to prescreen people based on their ages, locations, interests, professions, and other criteria. People commonly meet and have short dates at a coffee shop, which provides a chance to see the person face-to-face and is the perfect venue for brief meetings.

If things work out on the coffee date, you might get together at another time for dinner or a day event. If you want to break into online dating gradually, just scan through the sites before you jump in. That way, you can get an idea of who you might meet and what it could be like. A friend of mine scanned sites for months before she finally had the courage to go on a date.

Don't get discouraged. Some people put up old pictures, lie about their weight, height, career, age, and so on. You may have to go on many coffee dates before you find someone interesting. Proceed cautiously, and stay focused on the goal of what you what. Many couples I know have found happy, lifelong relationships with wonderful people they never would've met if they hadn't done online dating.

Cynthia, who was about fifty-five when her husband died, was very selective in screening men online before dating. She began her search for a companion about one year after her husband died suddenly. In fact, she hadn't even considered dating until I told her, "Cynthia, you've probably got another thirty years or so left to live. Do you really want to spend those next thirty years alone?" She narrowed her search down to two men who fit her high standards and ultimately went on several dates with them before choosing Jeremy, a successful, kind, intelligent entrepreneur.

After they had dated about six months, Cynthia introduced him to her children, who adored Jeremy. After a few years, they moved in together and built a welcoming home that's enjoyed by both of their families. Cynthia and Jeremy have traveled the world together and with many family members. Cynthia's children think of Jeremy as a true father figure, and he has been able to fulfill that role while continuing to recognize the importance of their father, who passed away.

It has been exciting to see how Cynthia rebuilt her life with a wonderful man and established a new career. This match might have never happened if it weren't for online dating.

EXPERIENCING THE POWER OF TRAVEL

Traveling is a good way to discover the new you. There may be places you always wanted to visit, but your partner or spouse wasn't interested. Now is the time to take those trips and learn about different cultures, see historic or scenic locations, and experience new venues and meals. Where you go depends on your budget, the amount of time you can spend, and your interests.

Even just a brief trip can provide the opportunity to relax and reflect on the changes in your life and plans for the future. If you're on a tight budget, consider going somewhere within driving distance. Perhaps you're near a city and can take advantage of museums and parks. If you have friends or family in the area that you choose to visit, you may enjoy staying with them.

There are also a variety of discounts available for hotels if you need lodging. You'll also be more likely to reduce the costs of travel if you plan to visit during the off-peak season or schedule your trip well in advance of the day you arrive.

Do you like solitude and just want to get away some place? Maybe you just need to hunker down in a quiet room with a good book and then take a walk and enjoy beautiful scenery. If your budget includes a hotel visit, look for places near beaches, parks, lakes, or other natural attractions.

Traveling with friends can be fun. If you organize a trip as a group, you can split the cost of a hotel or suite and enjoy catching up. Your good friends can help you to feel better, smile, and laugh. A few of my friends from college got together and planned a weekend trip to the desert to help one of our longtime friends cope with a loss. We had been friends for forty years, and it was like having a slumber party for grownups.

Day Trip Checklist

If you don't have much time to travel, never underestimate the fun you can experience by taking a day trip. If you plan to drive, think about events or locales to visit. Maybe you'll drive to the city to see a play or go to a museum, or you'll experience the joy of hiking. Whether you take these jaunts by yourself or with friends, you may be surprised how exciting it can be to get away from your day-to-day routine and try something new.

Here's a checklist of short excursions that can provide just what you need without breaking the bank:

- Aquariums
- Art exhibits
- Beaches
- Comedy shows
- Concerts
- Farmer's markets
- Festivals
- Gardens
- Home tours
- Lakes
- Local attractions and historic sites
- Movies
- Museums
- Parks
- Plays
- Public or miniature golf courses
- Seminars
- Spas
- Sporting events
- Wineries

If you're comfortable going on group excursions, contact your local city chamber of commerce to see what types of day trips are available. Transportation may be provided, and you'll also meet other people while you're there. Many senior centers also offer day trips. Check it out!

If you have more time and a bigger budget, consider taking a trip to a place you've never been before, and create some new memories.

You can do this alone, with a new partner (if you are ready), or with friends or family members.

> Samantha decided to take a road trip to visit art galleries in Sedona, Santa Fe, and Taos, about six months after her husband died. It was something she had always wanted to do, but it never materialized because her husband wasn't interested in art. Samantha was nervous because she rarely traveled alone when she was married. She spent a lot of time planning the two-week trip by searching the internet for places to visit.
>
> Samantha discovered that the trip was just what she needed to relax. She liked the freedom of being on her own schedule, discovering new types of artwork, finding quaint places to eat meals, and reading or watching her favorite Netflix series at night. Plus, it gave her a chance to get away from her routine at home and simply relax.

I also have discovered the joy of visiting new venues. I had heard about the Shakespeare Festival in Ashland, Oregon, for many years but never had the chance to experience it. Jack and I drove there and stayed at a charming B&B, where we met interesting people. It was my first road trip from Santa Cruz to Oregon, and I enjoyed the beautiful scenery and lush trees along the way. It was the type of adventure that I would have enjoyed, even if I had traveled alone.

The town of Ashland was charming, and I felt like I'd stepped back in time to my college days. I was surrounded by aging hippies. People say that my hometown of Santa Cruz is retro, but Ashland is even more so. I imagined that this endearing little town that's known for its annual Shakespeare Festival looked exactly the same as it did back in the '60s and '70s.

This was also the first time I had visited a B&B where I really got to know the people who stayed there. We shared breakfast at a large table and talked about the plays we watched the night before. In the evening, we joined the same group of people for tea and dessert to discuss our interpretations of the plays we had just seen. This experience made me realize that I had merely scratched the surface of places to create positive memories going forward.

Exploring new places with other family members or friends can be fun, too. I was fortunate enough to take a long vacation with my daughter, Laura, and Megan, my stepdaughter, almost two years after Paul died. I didn't want them to think of the winter holidays as another time spent without their dad. I wanted to change the dynamics of the season and create an entirely new experience for the three of us.

Our first big trip was such an exciting adventure. Laura was a freshman in college, and Megan was seven years older. During this trip, I noticed that the age gap between the two of them had shrunk, and I could see that they had become closer. We visited historic sites, museums, charming cafés, and shops.

The waiter at one restaurant decided that we should sit at a table occupied by a cat, who had a bed right next to my chair. We must have looked like people who would welcome cats at the dinner table. Since we missed our cat, who was at home, the seating arrangement, although unconventional, was fine for us.

I got up the courage to see a play on my own while the girls explored other venues. This may sound like a no-brainer, but if you've never attended a play alone, you may understand why I considered this a big step toward independence. It was a turning point for me to feel comfortable enough to attend the play alone.

Paul would've been amazed that the three of us traveled for ten days in tight quarters and didn't have one argument. It was a great time of bonding.

A few years later, we were fortunate enough to visit Italy. Megan spoke Italian, so she was the interpreter on that trip. We walked everywhere, rode bikes through the walled town of Luca, ate pizza and gelato every day in Florence, and saw historic buildings, the Roman Colosseum, churches, museums, and wineries. Paul and I had always planned to visit Italy. Although he didn't live long enough for us to take this trip together, I felt that he was with us in spirit and was able to experience his own joy through the eyes of his daughters.

When your spouse of partner dies, traveling changes. The romantic trips you had expected to take with him or her are no longer possible. But my experience—and that of many other people who have traveled after a loss—has shown that there are so many opportunities to explore and discover more about the world around you. Be open to these experiences, if you have the time and budget and are physically able to travel.

Cruises are a great way to travel, although some of them can be costly. My experience is very limited and brings back memories of being incredibly seasick, but most people find cruises as a great way to travel with friends, family, or alone. Some companies specialize in singles' cruises and activities onboard, so that everything is taken care of for you, including mass quantities of delicious food and all types of entertainment, recreational activities, and tours.

Traveling can be comforting and eye-opening. If you've lost a loved one, and you want to simply get away and try a new experience, consider a trip as an adventure to look forward to and enjoy. Online resources and travel agents can provide details about the types of trips available, based on your requirements and budget, including day trips.

In summary, while the loss of your loved one is painful, you can take steps to rebuild your life and discover new relationships and experiences to help you cope and thrive. You can't change the past, but by getting to know the new you, it's possible to find positive ways to shape your future.

CHAPTER 5

▼

FEELING BETTER OVER TIME

As I've mentioned, the first year after losing your loved one can be very difficult, but don't expect the loss to fade away quickly after that period. You'll have constant triggers, and coping with them should get easier over time. Everyone's circumstance is different. Here are some typical scenarios, based on year two and beyond, and some recommendations to help you. (Details about getting through the first year are discussed at the end of the appendix.)

KNOWING WHAT TO EXPECT

Many people join grief groups after the first year, especially if they still feel overwhelmed and sad and haven't worked through the tasks of grief. For example:

> When Helen, who was Brenda's longtime partner, died, Brenda simply accelerated the pace of her routines and activities, instead of taking time to process her grief. She worked more than ten hours a day and joined so many groups that there was little time to reflect on her loss. Just two weeks after Helen's death, Brenda started a major remodeling project on

her home, which was impulsive and disruptive and added to her stress level.

It wasn't until year two, when Brenda's friends advised her to get some help, that she finally allowed the loss to finally sink in and joined a grief group. Through her involvement with the group, Brenda realized that she needed to reduce distractions and take the time to grieve.

Most people who put some effort into healing during the first year will be in better shape to set long-term goals later on. They've already done some of the hard work in processing grief. The long-term goals they set can expand upon the efforts they've made during the first year. These goals may be related to their aspirations, living situation, finances, health, and relationships.

At the end of this book's appendix, you'll see an example of how to develop a plan for the first year. By year two and beyond, you should determine which adjustments need to be made once you've gotten through the key milestones and had a chance to deal with estate- and tax-related issues. You may have begun to develop some new interests, activities, and friends. The table on the next page includes sample goals from the first year and goals and actions for year two and beyond.

SAMPLE PLAN—ESTABLISHING AND FOCUSING ON LONG-TERM PRIORITIES

YEAR ONE GOALS	YEAR TWO AND BEYOND GOALS	YEAR TWO AND BEYOND ACTIONS
Stay mentally and physically healthy.	Stay mentally and physically healthy and increase activities that will support this goal.	• If needed, seek professional counseling and join a grief group if you didn't do this during the first year. • Attend a class in a topic of interest and actively participate in community workshops for personal growth. • Exercise at least five days a week. • Identify a target weight and focus on diet and nutrition to reach and maintain that goal. • Make sure to get checkups, tests, and vaccines, based on your doctor's recommendations.
Take control of your finances and develop a financial plan.	Take control of your finances and implement a financial plan.	Look at your investments and income, and identify the amount of income you'll need each year to support your expenses. Make adjustments in a timely manner to ensure a secure future: • If you like living in your home but cannot support it on one income for an extended period, consider options, such as renting out a room. • If you decide that it's time to relocate and downsize or to relocate to be closer to family, friends, or employment opportunities, do your research and set a feasible target date for relocation. • If you're not working but need additional income, look into full-time or part-time employment. If you have a business network, seek the help of people you know. If not, begin to search online for opportunities and explore community resources that can help you. If you want to learn a new skill or start a job in an area where you lack expertise, consider doing volunteer work in that field to help build up your experience. • If you have disabilities or need public assistance, contact your local city government offices to find out what resources are available to you. • Update your estate plan.

YEAR ONE GOALS	YEAR TWO AND BEYOND GOALS	YEAR TWO AND BEYOND ACTIONS
Visit with friends and family more often.	Visit with friends and family more often.	• Identify a target number of days per month or quarter that you will visit with friends and family, and contact them to arrange visits. • Join a community group from your place of worship or other organization.
If you have a job, try not to take on more work than you can handle.	Consider expanding your career opportunities if you're working and your current position isn't meeting your objectives.	If your current position isn't providing the income, benefits, or challenge that you expected, set a target date for looking into your options. This could be applying for other jobs in your company, getting training to learn a new skill, or looking at outside job opportunities.
Take a music class and join a local choir.	Take a music class and join a local choir. Consider pursuing other hobbies.	Continue singing in the choir and taking classes, as desired. If you have other hobbies you want to pursue, then identify what they are and set a date when you will be ready to get involved.
Identify what makes you happy and gives you something to look forward to doing.	Identify what makes you happy and gives you something to look forward to doing. Implement a plan to make these activities a reality.	The first year after a loss can be chaotic and cause you to be conflicted or confused. You may have tried different things to make you happy, only to discover that they were just Band-Aid solutions to satisfy immediate cravings for comfort. By now, you should be able to think more clearly about what changes you need to make on your path to happiness. • Set some clear long-term goals, and develop and implement a plan to reach them.
Take some day trips with a friend.	Put a comprehensive travel plan into action.	Identify places you'd like to visit. Plan a trip based on your interests and budget, and then take it.
	Volunteer (new goal).	Volunteer to participate in a local charity. Identify a cause or causes that are important to you. Determine how many hours you can contribute to that organization each month, and set a date when you can join that group as a volunteer.

Once you've developed these long-term goals, take out a calendar (I prefer one that has plenty of space for each day so that I can add notes), set target dates, and identify what you are going to do throughout the year to reach these goals. Objectives that go into the following year can be carried over in a separate calendar. Although you may not be able to accomplish everything, do what's reasonable. Just keep in mind that you can't reach your destination without a map. Let your calendar be your map.

Stephen Covey, the author of *The 7 Habits of Highly Effective People*, once said, "Begin with the end in mind." Take that approach. By understanding your priorities and setting incremental goals, you can expedite healing and experience happiness, fulfillment, and growth.

▼

CHAPTER 6

Navigating Your Way through New Relationships and Beginnings

SETTING EXPECTATIONS BASED ON YOUR AGE, SITUATION, ECONOMIC FACTORS, AND GENDER

In this chapter, I'll describe some examples of the grief journey that people have experienced and the ways they were able to move forward, based on their ages at the time of the loss, personal situation, economic factors, and gender.

If you've lost a spouse or partner when your own expected lifespan is another fifteen to sixty years, you're generally more likely to become involved in a new, permanent relationship than someone with less time ahead—but there certainly are exceptions. Someone who is eighty years old or older and interested in finding love again and makes it a priority also has opportunities for starting a new relationship. People in this demographic may enjoy having a companion for social activities but generally are less likely to actively seek out a more serious relationship. Instead, many people in their eighties may decide to build upon their friendships, hobbies, and interests and to spend more time with their families.

If your spouse or partner died of a long-term illness, you may be reluctant to put yourself in another situation where you once again could be forced to deal with the pain of loss. With this in mind, some people, consciously or unconsciously, tend to select new partners that are "right for now."

It may take time before they allow themselves to experience true love again, assuming they had a fulfilling relationship with the person who died. In these cases, their initial new partners may be a transitional partner. They may be so happy to have a companion that they are not aware that the person they're spending time with is fine for now but not for the long-term.

I had two relationships after Paul died. I didn't realize it at the time, but now I'm aware that these were transitional partners. When I started dating Jack, which was more than nine years after Paul's death, I felt an instant trust and connection that evolved into love. We sometimes finished each other's sentences and knew each other's thoughts. My family embraced him, and his family did the same with me. My friends became his, and his friends became mine. He has an amazing sense of humor and intellect, traits that he shared with Paul. As I got to know Jack even better, I realized that I wanted to be with him forever. I cast aside my fear of loving so deeply again and opened my heart to Jack.

Your desire to start a new relationship may also depend on the one you had with your spouse or partner before he or she died. What you're looking for in a new partner at your present stage of life might be different than what you wanted when you were with the person you're grieving.

Some of the widows I've known were married a long time to their husbands, and over the years, their relationships had soured due to issues like infidelity, alcoholism, or just by growing apart. These women still loved their late husbands but wanted to make sure they didn't repeat mistakes of the past in any future relationship.

Older widows and widowers may not be interested in seeking a new partner, but they enjoy having companions when they go to events, movies, restaurants, parties, and other activities.

- If Jane likes to stay up and read until midnight and wake up at 8:00 a.m., she may not want to live with Scott, who goes to sleep at 9:30 p.m. and wakes at 6:00 a.m. each day.

- If Peggy is frugal, and Harry spends significantly more than he can afford, this could be a sign that these two people shouldn't live together.

- If your families don't get along with your new partner, there could be more problems ahead, and it's best to proceed cautiously.

We all have our routines and priorities, and they become more ingrained as we age. Set your expectations for the type of relationship you want to have, based on what's most important to you and how much you are willing to compromise. A widow or widower may have an enjoyable, steady relationship with someone but chooses not to live with that person because of conflicting values, priorities, or other circumstances.

> We all have our routines and priorities, and they become more ingrained as we age.

Some people may decide they'd rather pursue their passions—such as art, music, reading, gardening, writing, or sports—than get involved with someone new. They might also prefer to expand their network of friends to provide a more satisfying social structure and stave off loneliness.

Men and women handle the rebuilding process differently. Women tend to gravitate toward grief groups, therapy, and activities that facilitate sharing their loss on the path to healing. Statistically, men are less likely to share their feelings as openly because they don't want to appear weak.

Here are some general examples of the path to healing people take, based on their age at the time of their loss.

Ages Twenty through Thirty-Nine

Losing someone when you are in your twenties or thirties is devastating, but due to their potential longevity, people in this age group may, in time, be more likely to remarry or establish a long-term partnership than someone much older. After all, they could live another sixty or more years, so why spend that much time alone if they prefer to be coupled?

If they have a child or children, they may yearn to have a suitable father or mother figure enter their lives. If they don't have children, this might be an opportunity to have the family they always wanted. Of course, entering into a new relationship, especially when it involves blending families, takes effort, understanding, and patience. Many people, however, are willing to take that leap to find love and happiness again. Here's an example:

> Fred married his college sweetheart, Sheryl, when he was twenty-nine. They built a wonderful life together, moved around the country, and had exciting jobs. After they'd been married for about four years, they decided to have children. Sheryl wasn't able to conceive because she had ovarian cysts. After additional testing, they discovered she had ovarian cancer.
>
> During the first year of Sheryl's diagnosis, Fred began the grieving process and spent considerable time in denial. He did everything he could to support her, keep her comfortable, and try to help her heal. He moved on to acceptance when he realized that the surgery and chemo would no longer help and that she wasn't going to live.
>
> Sheryl fought the battle with cancer for three years with chemotherapy and surgery, but she couldn't win. Eventually, hospice provided comfort care for her in their home, with Fred by her side. When she passed, Fred felt a deep loss, but he also was relieved that she would no longer suffer.
>
> Fred accepted that his life would start on a new path and that at age thirty-nine, he still had many

years ahead of him. What gave him this strength? Fred attributes it to struggling through different "chapters" in his life.

His first big chapter involved several years in the military during the Vietnam War. The last two years were unbearable, and he sometimes doubted that he could get through that ordeal, but he survived. His next big chapter challenge was focused on completing college while working part-time. Fred felt that because he'd made it through college and had survived the rigors of war, he could pull himself through the chapter of loss.

He wasn't interested in attending grief groups. His mom and close friend were with Fred when Sheryl passed, but he wanted to keep his grief personal and deal with it on his own terms and at his own pace. He had done all that he could to help Sheryl, so Fred didn't experience survivor's guilt, which happens to many people.

Fred became very involved in his work as an engineer to help pass the time, pay the bills, and provide the much-needed structure in his life. After several months, he decided he was ready to socialize and went to a community event for singles. There, he met a woman who said she'd like to set up Fred on a blind date with her close friend, Wendy. (Keep in mind that this was how many people met each other before there were personal ads and online dating services.)

Fred never expected to begin a new relationship—he wasn't looking for one —but when he met Wendy, he was drawn to her for many reasons. Wendy was attractive, compassionate, honest, interesting, and intelligent.

Fred and Wendy fell in love and now have been happily married for many years. He has no regrets about meeting her soon after Sheryl died, and he had no desire to date anyone else before settling down. Fred had married Sheryl when he was thirty and had dated enough women before meeting Sheryl that he knew what he wanted in a partner. Wendy met all of his expectations and more. He also got along well with Wendy's young daughter. Fred and Wendy had a son a few years after they were married. Fred's new path brought him happiness, healing, and a family.

Ages Forty through Fifty-Nine

In your forties and fifties, you may still have kids at home. You're not only dealing with your own loss, but you also have to recognize what your children are going through and give them the support they need. (This can be the case with other age groups as well.) Even if your children are grown and out of the house, they likely will grapple with their loss and may not understand changes in your behavior, because they may be focused on their own suffering. To compound the challenge, if you introduce a new partner to them too soon, they can feel betrayed and hurt and may not comprehend your struggles and needs.

Tina, a fifty-year-old office manager, was with her husband, Josh, and thirteen-year-old son, Eric, on a cruise, when Josh died suddenly and unexpectedly. Josh, who wasn't used to exercising, overdid it on the second day of the cruise, when the boat landed, by taking a long hike on a hot day. Josh returned to the ship feeling uncomfortable and out of breath, but he didn't think it was a problem. He ate a big dinner that night and went back to the cabin, where he had a sudden heart attack in front of Eric and Tina. Although they called for help, the ship's doctor wasn't able to save him. Both Tina and Josh had to live with the memory of that horrific day and their feelings of helplessness.

When they returned home, Tina was inundated with paperwork and despair as she tried to cope with life without Josh. To compound the stress, Josh had run his own auto shop with six employees, and Tina had to determine how she could possibly run the business without him. She was his manager, but taking on the role of owner required more effort and skills than she had anticipated.

Although Tina wanted to attend a grief group and see a therapist, she considered both options a luxury of time that she didn't have. She made excuses and said she had too many responsibilities to think about self-care. Instead, Tina threw herself into her work. Meanwhile, Eric's grades dropped dramatically. He spent far too much time online, began to withdraw from his friends, and started drinking alcohol.

Tina was overwhelmed. The loss of her husband and shock of his sudden death caused Tina great anxiety. She had trouble sleeping at night and was worried about how she could possibly keep the business going, pay the bills, and deal with her loneliness.

It wasn't until she got into a car accident that she realized she needed to get help. Tina had been distracted, didn't notice a red light, and crashed into the car in front of her. Fortunately, no one was injured in the accident, but it was just one more stress factor at a time when her coping skills were eroding.

Tina signed up for one-on-one grief support at her local hospice. By attending that program, she realized that she was not alone. Tina learned that she needed a plan to understand how the loss impacted her so that she could put her life back together successfully and steer her son in the right direction. With the help of a grief counselor, Tina learned how to release the guilt of not being able to save her husband's life.

She also learned that it was important to go easy on herself and set realistic expectations regarding her priorities and actions. Ultimately, she sold the business to one of the senior managers at the shop and decided to take courses to become a realtor, a career she preferred and one that she could begin in her fifties.

The grief counselor also convinced Tina to enroll Eric in a program for teens to help him deal with loss.

> The grief counselor also convinced Tina to enroll Eric in a program for teens to help him deal with loss.

Eric learned coping strategies and met new friends in that group who shared a common bond with him that people who hadn't gone through losing a parent might not understand. His grades improved, and he stopped drinking alcohol.

About one year after Josh died, Tina decided it was time to begin socializing. She wasn't ready for a long-term relationship. She just wanted a companion. Tina met several men online and eventually started going out with John. Although John initially appeared to be patient and friendly, Eric resented him, and they had frequent clashes.

John, who was divorced and had a daughter, got along well with Tina, but he was jealous of the time that Tina spent with Eric. John began making many suggestions on how Tina should manage her son. Eventually, this situation eroded their relationship as a couple, and Tina broke up with John after six months.

Over the next year, Tina went on numerous group outings and coffee dates, but nothing ever really clicked with the men she met. She had a much better time visiting with her friends and family. She found herself comparing each man she met to Josh, and no one could measure up.

For many months, Tina would take her dog, a fox terrier, to a local dog park to relax. She got to know the people who visited the park regularly and became friendly with Brian, who also had a terrier. Brian was a mortgage broker, and most of the time they would talk about their dogs and the real estate business. Tina noticed that she was beginning to feel very comfortable talking with Brian. When he asked her if she'd go to lunch with him, she thought, *Why not?* Tina assumed they could talk about business, and he'd be a good contact.

It hadn't occurred to Tina that she would eventually fall in love with Brian, but that's what happened.

After all, she wasn't looking for a relationship, and Brian didn't look like her typical type. Brian was short, thin, and bald, and Tina always went for men who were tall, heavier, and had lots of hair. Still, there was something about him that she couldn't identify that seemed familiar, endearing, and safe. They started going to movies together, out to dinner, and to plays, but she kept him at a distance because she just wasn't ready to get involved. Brian patiently followed her cues, and eventually, their relationship blossomed into one that was loving, caring, and romantic.

Tina waited until she had known Brian for four months before introducing him to Eric. Brian had been married briefly when he was younger but never had children, although he was very devoted to his nephews and treated them like sons.

Brian and Eric clicked from the start. They both liked baseball, and Brian asked if he could watch Eric play for his local team. Sometimes Eric and Brian would watch a science-fiction film at the movies. They'd talk about sports, politics, trends, and school. Tina realized that with Brian, she was gaining not just a wonderful partner for herself but also someone who could be like a father to Eric.

Eventually, Brian and Tina got married, and they built a life together with common goals and values. Although Tina loved her home, she wanted a fresh start to create new memories. Brian's home was nice, but it was in a more isolated part of town. Tina wanted to be near parks, restaurants, and shopping. They decided to sell their houses, combine their resources and buy a new place together.

They blended their businesses and helped raise and motivate Eric, who went on to college and became a teacher. Although Eric would always miss Josh, he also thought of Brian as a dad and was grateful to have him in his life.

Ages Sixty through Seventy-Nine

People in their sixties and seventies today often lead a lifestyle that may be more active and healthier than the lifestyle their parents experienced. For example, their parents were raised at a time when smoking was not considered a health hazard. I've heard people say that seventy is the "new" fifty. That sounds good to me!

Many health breakthroughs that weren't available to their parents have helped the boomers to expand their longevity and the quality of life. With a good diet, exercise, and self-care, you're more likely to live longer and feel younger. That's why it's common for people in this age group to form new relationships in their sixties and seventies after losing a spouse or partner.

One of the advantages of reaching sixty is that you likely have a better understanding of who you are and what you want at this point in your life. You may have already accomplished goals that you established earlier, whether it's career objectives, owning a home, spending time with your friends or adult children and grandchildren (if you have them), focusing on volunteer work, or other priorities that really matter. Having this insight about your own interests and values can enable you to be more selective as you determine what you want to do. If you're seeking another relationship, you're more likely to know what to look for at this time in your life. Here's an example:

Donna and her husband, Steve, got married when they were in their late thirties. He was an accountant, and she taught third grade. They didn't have children, but they both enjoyed an active social life with friends and often hiked together on the weekends. When Steve was sixty-four, he died from complications after a skiing accident when he and Donna were on vacation. Donna wasn't a skier, so she wasn't present when the accident happened.

Steve was in the hospital for several days before he developed a severe infection that quickly caused his body to shut down.

For several months after his death, Donna just wanted to stay at home. Steve died six months after Donna had retired from teaching, so she not only lost her husband, but her career had just recently ended. She stopped exercising and lost her appetite. She struggled with sleep, and rarely answered the phone or looked at her mail. Donna had a large circle of friends but only a small group of family members that included two cousins, a sister-in-law, and a niece, all of whom lived three thousand miles away.

About three months after Steve died, Donna decided that she was ready to seek help. She signed up for a grief group at her local hospice and began attending church on Sundays. The grief group provided much-needed structure to her life, which included a place she had to be once a week, along with people who would understand her loss and help her to complete incremental goals. Her Sunday visits to church also gave Donna an opportunity to be around people in a healing environment.

When Steve died, several of Donna's close friends tried to reach out to her. But Donna wasn't ready to share her loss with them and rarely socialized. After attending several grief group sessions and church visits, she finally realized that if she was going to heal, she had to accept the help and companionship of her friends. Donna needed to come to terms with what she wanted and planned to do for this phase of her life. Steve didn't get the chance to live another twenty or thirty years with her. She realized that time was limited, and she owed it to him—and herself—to make the most out of life.

Donna decided that she needed to get out more and give herself permission to experience joy again. She would plan routine visits with friends, exercise on a regular basis, take a pottery class, and work part-time as a substitute teacher. Getting back into the workplace, even just two days a week, gave Donna a sense of purpose and provided extra income to supplement her retirement. Although Steve had some life insurance, and together they had a modest savings, Donna knew that she would now be responsible for her financial future on her own. Going back to work helped to address that challenge.

Once Donna got through the financial hurdles and was back into a routine, she thought about what it would be like to have a companion. She had to convince herself that she wasn't replacing Steve—he was a unique person, and she would always hold his memories in her heart. Instead, she considered the possibility that there was someone else out there she would enjoy spending time and getting to know. She missed sharing cozy dinners at home by the fireplace, walking on the beach, and having someone to hug.

Before Steve's accident, Donna said she always felt young at heart. So why couldn't she start over? The next step was trying to figure out how to make this happen. The thought of dating at sixty-four was scary!

One of Donna's friends, Laurie, recommended that she set up a profile on an online dating site for people her age. She took Donna's picture and helped her to write a profile. If it weren't for Laurie's encouragement, Donna would've found an excuse to avoid online dating.

When she narrowed her search to a few people who seemed interesting, including a man who was a widower, Donna went on coffee dates. A few of them were disappointing and awkward. One man talked the whole time with food in his mouth. Another looked at least fifteen years older than his picture. Laurie insisted that Donna shouldn't give up. She said the odds were in her favor. Besides, each experience gave Donna more confidence and brought her one step closer to finding the right match.

The fifth man Donna met, Carter, was intriguing. He was genuine, humble, smart, and athletic. Carter was a divorced high school teacher and was semiretired. What impressed Donna most was his sense of humor and warmth. They shared the same religion, hobbies, and interests.

After maintaining a relationship for two years, Donna decided to move in with Carter, whose mortgage was paid off, and keep her home as a rental unit. While they discussed marriage, there were several economic reasons why it made sense to remain as committed partners instead. They met with an accountant and worked out a plan to have an equitable financial arrangement outside of marriage. For example, although Carter's stepson from a prior marriage would inherit a portion of the house, Donna had a life estate arrangement that allowed her to stay there as long as she wanted, if she were to outlive Carter.

It has been fifteen years since they met, and they enjoy their life together. They often comment that they feel like young teenagers in love. Donna is convinced that because she loved Steve so deeply, she knew what it meant to be in love. Carter honors and respects the relationship Donna had with Steve, while sharing a new and different life with her.

Eighties and Beyond

When you're in your eighties, and you lose your spouse or partner, you may feel how lucky you were to have enjoyed each other for so long. That's looking at the situation from a positive perspective. On the other hand, if you've spent most of your life with your spouse or partner, it's very difficult to imagine life without this person.

Many of the seniors I've met had married their spouses when they were in their late teens or early twenties. Some of the women of that generation never worked outside the home. They raised their families and took care of the meals and social activities but often delegated handling the finances to their husbands. Suddenly, they were faced with making financial decisions that were new to them at a time in their lives when they felt particularly vulnerable. Their husbands were frequently the ones who took care of home repairs, carried out the trash, and so on.

The women I've met tended to handle their loss better if they had a good support system of friends, family, or religious community. Many of them relied on their adult children to help them as they navigated their way through the grief process and gradually assumed some of the tasks handled by their husbands. Keep in mind that these women, like men, also had to deal with their own health issues, like problems with mobility, hearing, and vision, which tend to compound as you get older. These problems happened to them at the same time they had to cope with the loss of their loved ones.

Men in their eighties and beyond generally took on the role of the key financial provider but were less likely to cook, do laundry, clean up, and plan social activities. They also were less likely to seek outside help, such as attending grief groups or seeing therapists. Many of them tended to rely on their families, when possible, to provide much-needed support.

My father had no idea how to cook. When he was in his fifties, even the microwave was a challenge to him. His generation was different from mine (baby boomers), Gen X, and other younger generations, who are much more likely to share household responsibilities.

People who lose their loved ones in their eighties and beyond likely have to take on new roles and responsibilities that once were delegated to their spouses or partners. They're also more likely to have other losses that are not as often experienced by prior generations. Their friends may have passed away. Or they had to stop driving, which can represent a loss of independence. They may resent having to rely on their children for help, and they may have health issues that can impact their mobility and quality of life.

What's especially difficult is having to leave their familiar homes because the level of upkeep is too much to handle alone. They may also have to move to a senior facility, or relocate and leave their existing social network behind to be closer to family members.

> What's especially difficult is having to leave their familiar homes because the level of upkeep is too much to handle alone.

By the time you're in your eighties and nineties, you're less likely to seek out a new, serious coupled relationship because you realize your time is more limited. Fortunately, there are many things you can still do to make the most out of each day. Here's an example:

Rachel was eighty-two when her husband, Adam, died of complications from Alzheimer's. She and Adam had raised three daughters, who all lived two thousand miles away. Rachel and Adam retired in their late sixties and enjoyed the night life of Chicago and the activities in the city.

By the time Adam was seventy-eight, he started experiencing memory loss. He became quiet when they socialized, withdrew from activities, and was under a doctor's care. Rachel cut back on social events but tried to make sure that she and Adam went out for meals occasionally and took walks together. One night he left the house in his bathrobe and wandered through the neighborhood and couldn't remember where he lived. What made matters worse was that he exited through a window, not a door.

After that incident, Rachel met with her doctor and decided to put Adam in an elder care facility, where he would be safe. Rachel was dealing her own health issues—diabetes and hypertension—but tried to keep those conditions under control and focus on Adam. It was painful to see the man who was once so vital and sharp lose the ability to communicate effectively and process information. Still, she visited him each day and cherished the times when he would smile or utter something that sparked a pleasant memory. When he passed, Rachel missed him dearly, but she also felt a sense of relief because she knew that Adam hadn't wanted to live that way.

The medical costs for Adam's care took a huge chunk out of what had once been a large retirement fund. Rachel had to cope with the loss and make major financial decisions. She sold her home and most of her belongings, other than the items that her daughters wanted to keep, and relocated to Florida to be near them and her grandchildren. It was very difficult for Rachel to leave her friends and the house that she loved when she moved to Florida.

Her oldest daughter, Sarah, invited Rachel to move in with their family. Rachel declined because she liked being independent. So she moved into a one-bedroom apartment in a senior-living facility near Sarah's family.

Even though it was a big change and not the way she had ever intended to spend her final years, Rachel established goals for her new life. She made it a point to meet new people at her senior home, which had more than one hundred residents. Instead of eating meals alone in her apartment, for example, she went to the cafeteria for lunch and dinner. The facility had bus trips to movies, plays, museums, and other activities that Rachel attended.

Over time, she met several new friends, male and female, who joined her for meals and some of the events. She didn't let her impaired mobility keep her from enjoying these activities. She got around by using a walker, and her hearing aids made it possible to join in conversations without feeling that she was missing out.

Rachel was surprised at how easy it was to meet people. She also volunteered to participate in a weekly cooking program, in which some residents at her senior center prepared meals that were taken to a local homeless shelter. She loved to cook and found a new sense of accomplishment in being able to provide a service to her new community.

Rachel attended religious services weekly with her daughter and visited her grandchildren at least once or twice a week. While she missed Adam terribly, Rachel was comforted by knowing that she could spend more time with her family now that she had relocated. Rachel shared stories about Adam with her children and grandchildren and kept his memory alive. Over time, by thinking about everything that made their relationship so special and talking about the good times, the images of Adam during his illness faded away and were replaced with happy memories.

CHAPTER 7

▼

LEARNING TO LOVE AGAIN

Love can take many forms, whether it's finding a new relationship, enjoying time with friends and family, or discovering a new hobby, volunteer activity, or career based on your passion. The conundrum is that people may know what they *don't* want, but they don't always know what they *do* want.

DECIDING IF YOU'RE READY FOR A NEW RELATIONSHIP

Let's take a closer look at what you really want to achieve in terms of a relationship. At first, you may think it would be great to have a new partner, but you're reluctant to live with anyone else because you might feel uncomfortable when someone encroaches on your space and starts bringing items and furniture into your home.

You might like to get up early, and it bothers you that your partner sleeps late. You could resent having to purchase groceries for food you don't eat. It annoys you just knowing that your partner would spend time in front of the TV during the day, watching the news or sports, when that person should be working or spending time with you. You already have a family and may not have the emotional space or time to deal with your partner's troubled daughter or sick mother.

What does this scenario tell you? Perhaps you're not ready for a new serious relationship because it requires too much emotional and possibly financial flexibility your part. If that's the case, it's time to hit the pause button and approach dating very slowly. Relationships are give-and-take. If you're not willing to compromise, you may be with the wrong person, the timing isn't right, or deep down inside, you really don't want a deep relationship—at least not now. Don't worry. It doesn't mean that you can't find a loving relationship again. You just need to determine what it is that you really want and need.

Let's say that you're willing to be flexible in some areas because you met someone who sparks your interest. This could be a great opportunity, but you still need to proceed carefully. If you don't know what you want in terms of a commitment or are simply reluctant to take any chances, then take your time. By not rushing into a relationship, you'll be better prepared and avoid getting into a situation you may later regret.

Ask yourself the following questions:

- Are you just looking for company—someone to attend certain events with you on a casual basis? If so, then make that known to the person you're seeing.
- Is that person willing to understand that you aren't ready for a serious relationship?
- Are you happy when you're with that individual?
- Do you feel comfortable and safe when you're with that person?
- Do your friends and/or family think this person is suitable for you?

If you answered yes to these questions, then you may be ready to spend time with this individual. You may also discover that you can start out as friends, and the relationship can build over time. Even if this arrangement never goes beyond the level of friendship, it could prepare you for how to interact when the right person comes along. As long as you are both honest with each other about your expectations, and you trust each other, it can be helpful to move slightly outside your comfort zone. Nothing ventured, nothing gained.

Let's assume that enough time has passed since your loss, and you've met someone that you would like to get to know better, someone who, at some point, could even be your future partner or spouse. Perhaps you met that person online, through a friend, at work, through your place of worship, or even serendipitously, such as when walking your dog or sitting in a restaurant. After a spending a reasonable amount of time together, you may be ready to introduce that person to your friends or family.

Keep in mind that your good friends want the best for you. They may be biased, particularly if they were close to your deceased loved one. However, pay attention to how they react when they see you with the new person in your life. You may be so smitten that you don't notice red flags, such as when the new guy spends most of the evening talking about himself and fails to show any interest in your friends. That's a sign that he is self-absorbed or lacks social skills.

However, if he passes this test, and if the two of you enjoy being together, then you may decide at some point to introduce him to your family. If your adult children, for example, seem to have reservations about him, ask them to tell you why. They may have good reasons, or they may simply be uncomfortable with the thought of their mom getting involved with someone other than their dad. If the new person meets your criteria for what you expect from a serious relationship, then you may need to get some counseling on how to deal with this new arrangement and make it successful.

BLENDING YOUR FAMILY AND MINE

Blending families can be a real blessing or a major challenge, so wait until you are at a point where you feel ready to discuss this issue with your future partner. If you get involved with someone new late in life, you each bring a certain amount of baggage to the table.

I've known widowers who were raising teenagers, for example, and had trouble with new relationships. The new women these men met didn't want to take on the responsibility of raising teens. These men ended the relationships and eventually found women who welcomed the opportunity to be part of their family.

The person you date (or have a serious relationship with) should understand and accept that your obligations and priorities to your family are very important. If the person cares for you as much as you care for him or her, then that individual will need to embrace your family too. If you're close to the family of your deceased spouse or partner, the new person in your life should respect that relationship as well.

The new person should also respect the relationship you had with your deceased spouse or partner. You may mention your former husband or wife from time to time, such as saying, "This was Tom's favorite restaurant," or "Louise loved to dance to that song too." After all, Tom or Louise may have been in your life for many years, and whatever you felt for that person hasn't gone away. It's natural that a memory of your spouse or partner will crop up in a conversation. You may even have a few pictures of them on the walls of your home or apartment.

The new love in your life needs to be comfortable enough to accept that your deceased spouse or partner helped shape you into who you are today and not be threatened by or jealous of that relationship. Conversely, it's important for you to be sensitive to the feelings of a new partner, so that this person doesn't feel like it's impossible to measure up to what you had in the past. It's a delicate balance and not always an easy one to manage. Make sure your new partner feels appreciated.

As mentioned earlier, Paul died in 2006. I still have certain rituals that I perform to honor him on his birthday. I contact Paul's family members on that day to see how they are doing. Jack accepts this as part of my past and understands that it doesn't take away from our relationship.

LIVING TOGETHER

When you get to the point where you and the new man or woman in your life can't stand being apart, it may be time to decide whether you want to live together or get married. Let's look at what this involves, starting with living together.

Moving in together is a big commitment, so give this decision a lot of thought. Let's say you've conquered the challenge of blending families and friends and are ready to take the next step. If you've met later in life, for example, you may each have your own home or apartment that you feel very comfortable in and don't want to leave.

Maybe you're currently living near your children, work, or friends, and your new partner lives an hour away from you. Deciding on where you should live together can present opportunities for starting anew or lead to financial and emotional issues that can break up your relationship. The checklist below should help you to make this decision.

Living Together Checklist

These are some questions to discuss with each other before you cohabitate:

- Where do you both prefer to live—in your partner's house or community or yours? Or would you both rather move elsewhere?
- Do both of you agree that you are totally committed to each other?
- If you both own homes, would you consider selling one of the homes or renting one out?
- Is selling one of the homes too big of a financial risk?

- How will moving in together impact the other important activities in your life—spending time with family and friends, working, and so on?
- How will each of you contribute to the household financially?
- Do you have similar tastes in decorating? If not, how will you work things out?
- If one of you owns the home, is that person willing to grant a life estate to the other one if the homeowner dies first? (This can be based on certain conditions. For example, the surviving partner can be responsible for paying the mortgage or buying the home if he or she prefers to stay there.)
- Have you identified all of the logistical changes that need to happen in order to live together?
- If the person moving into your home has too much furniture and other belongings, would a storage unit be an option?
- If your partner is leaving his or her long-term community to move in with you, what will you do to make that transition easier?

> *For example, how can you help your partner build friendships and get involved in your community?*

- What are your plans for accommodating overnight guests of your partner who is moving in?
- If your partner has a pet, what are your plans for accommodating the pet?
- If your partner is responsible for taking care of a family member who might need to move in as well, now or in the future, how well prepared are you to make this adjustment?

> *For example, Cindy moved into Tom's home, and two months later, Cindy's mom, Laurie, needed full-time care. Cindy couldn't afford a nursing home, so she moved her mom in with her and Tom. While Tom was sympathetic, having Laurie move in was more*

responsibility than Tom was prepared to deal with, and it resulted in the couple breaking up.

The same issue is also critical if you're moving children from one family into the home of another. Consider getting counseling before deciding to move in together to determine how this will impact your relationship and the children.

- Are you a night owl and your partner is a morning person? How will this impact your relationship on a long-term basis?
- Is one of you working and the other retired? What financial and emotional impact will this have on your relationship?
- What are the long-term goals of your relationship, and do you have mutual goals and values?

    For example, your partner may ultimately want to move to a remote location, while you enjoy living in the city. Are you both willing to be flexible on future goals?

- How do you each deal with money?

    If one of you spends freely and the other is very frugal, how will you make decisions about where to travel, how much to spend on each other, and so forth? Couples that have major disagreements about money are more likely to have problems. Be sure you have a plan to deal with these situations.

- Are you both willing to take care of each other if one of you has a major change in health?
- Is one of you sloppy and the other very neat and organized? If so, how are you going to address this issue?
- Do you plan to marry each other in the future?

> *If you both prefer to stay as partners, that's great. If both of you plan to marry each other in the future, the timing of the marriage may be an issue.*
>
> *If one of you has marriage in mind and the other doesn't, that's a problem. Marriage is a big decision. If your partner's long-term goals don't coincide with yours, then you may need counseling to determine whether the relationship will be successful. Don't assume you can change your partner's mind.*

Before you decide to move a partner into your home, look at how you each address small, everyday challenges, and see how important those are to you, as well as the big issues related to family, finances, and health. Successful relationships will always require a level of compromise. If there are too many things you want to change about that person, that's a red flag, even if these are not significant challenges.

Remember that it's a lot easier to have a relationship with someone you don't have to try to change. If you have differences, determine whether they are workable. For example, if you're a staunch conservative, and your new partner is a progressive liberal, you may decide to avoid discussing politics to keep your relationship on track. If you're super-organized and your partner is not, this doesn't have to be a deal-breaker. You can offer to take over certain organizational functions, such as tracking expenses, cleaning out the garage, putting dishes away after you remove them from the dishwasher, and so on.

TAKING THE BIG STEP—GETTING MARRIED

Remarrying isn't for everyone. But it may be just right for you if your new relationship is very strong, you've overcome most of the challenges discussed in the prior chapter about living together, and it makes the most sense from an emotional, spiritual, and financial standpoint. This doesn't mean that you need to have a short engagement. Take your time. Marriage is a big step, especially later in life, when you're bringing together multiple families and balancing the emotional and financial needs and expectations of young children, adult children, or even parents who may depend upon you.

When Jack proposed, I instantly knew that my response would be yes, even though I would've been okay with continuing our relationship as a couple without getting married. Marriage seemed the right option for me because I was in love with Jack, and it brought us closer together as a couple.

As an added bonus, we joined each other's social circles and expanded our wonderful friendships. Surprisingly, I invited a very close friend of mine and her husband to dinner one evening, and Jack invited his dear friends. It turned out they already knew each other very well and had been close friends for more than thirty years. What a blessing it was to discover that we had the same taste in friends!

Our wedding, which was simple but elegant, was truly one of the happiest days of my life. My sons proudly walked me down the aisle, and my granddaughters were the flower girls. My beloved stepfather, Shelly, and my mom danced up a storm on the dance floor. I was so happy to have friends and family together and share in this beautiful event. Sadly, Shelly died unexpectedly just three weeks after the wedding, but we will always have those memories of him being there to share such a beautiful, happy day.

You may wonder whether you can truly love someone deeply again after you lose your loved one. I can tell you from my experience—and from many people who have loved and lost—that yes, you can. It doesn't take away from what you had before. It's a way to build upon who you are now.

LOVING A NEW CAREER OR FULFILLING ACTIVITY

Not everyone is prepared or even interested in finding another spouse or partner. Many people are satisfied with pursuing other activities. Being on your own again gives you the opportunity to sort out your own identity, priorities, and passions—things you may have put on hold because you were too busy, served as a caretaker for your loved one, or hadn't considered exploring new options for rebuilding your life.

Tonya had always enjoyed writing, but she chose a career as a software developer because it seemed like a practical and lucrative field. She took some creative writing and poetry classes in high school and college and considered them a pleasant break from the math and science courses that her parents pressured her to pursue. She never fully enjoyed her job, which was her career up until she took a leave of absence at age sixty-five, following the death of her husband. Because working in the tech industry was lucrative, and Tonya had skills that were in demand, she had managed to accumulate a sizeable savings for her retirement.

After Jose died, Tonya didn't feel like returning to her unrelenting job that offered many perks. It took every last bit of energy she had, between training new staff members, traveling, commuting, and doing her own coding. Plus, her coworkers were all younger than her children. She wasn't motivated to participate in the after-hours social activities sponsored by her employer. Once she became eligible for Medicare, Tonya didn't have the financial pressure of worrying about health insurance. With these conditions in mind, Tonya was ready for a change.

Tonya's mortgage was paid off, and she was financially ready to retire. But what about her emotional state? She wondered whether it would be too difficult to leave her job, even one that she had outgrown, at a time when she was already facing the loss of her husband. Most grief counselors advise not to make any major changes until a year after your loss to avoid doing anything impulsive that you might later regret, but Tonya was determined to take on a new challenge.

Tonya loved pets and wanted to write books about how to raise and train animals and eventually get work experience as an animal trainer. She fostered a variety of dogs as hobby. She was ready to make a difference in a field that combined her desire to write with her interest in helping people take better care of their pets.

Tonya began her career incrementally by joining a meet-up group of local writers and researching dog-training best practices. She took a weekend workshop on how to develop and self-publish a book and became more active in her local community. She also took classes in animal training and volunteered to walk dogs for people with mobility disabilities, such as individuals who were recovering from injuries. It was important for her to create a structure where she'd have regular meetings, classes, and volunteer work, in addition to blocking out time to do her writing.

Of course, Tonya missed Jose tremendously, but she was ready to transform as she entered this new chapter in her life. It was the right time for her to make a change. The dramatic shift in her career—from software developer/manager to writer/animal trainer/volunteer—provided the creative satisfaction that she yearned for but had repressed for many years. Instead of commuting an average of three hours a day, she now had time to exercise and visit with friends.

As she became more involved in her multiple business activities, she expanded her social network. Tonya had lost the love of her life, but she blossomed in ways that were satisfying and that enabled her to find happiness.

ENJOYING THE COMPANY OF PETS, FAMILY, AND FRIENDS

Tonya's career transformation helped her get through a very difficult time, and her love of animals made that vision a reality. Don't underestimate the healing power that pets can provide as you cope with loss. Our furry friends can offer us owners an everyday presence of unconditional love.

When your spouse or partner is gone, it's difficult coming home to an empty house. I personally felt that when I walked in the door and was greeted by my dog, I was not alone. She was there to encourage me to take walks, watch TV with me, and stay by my side.

If you already have a pet that you consider a member of the family, you'll understand how being able to give and receive love from a pet is rewarding and comforting. Of course, pets are a big responsibility, and you'll need to make tradeoffs if you're considering getting one.

About a year after my dog died, I got a two-month-old puppy, Max. It was the first time I'd owned dog that was so young. I love him dearly, but the care involved initially reminded me of a scaled-down version of taking care of a baby. I had to dog-proof the house, "potty" train him, work with him to sleep through the night, and make sure that my time away from home was brief.

Of course, I also limited my travel during Max's transition period to his new home. If you're interested in having a dog but the responsibility is more than you can handle, consider getting an older one that is more independent and can be left alone for longer periods of time.

Many people have found that spending more time with their family and friends helps the healing process. For example, one widower I know watches his grandchildren after school each day. He developed a very close relationship with them, one that is very rewarding for him and the grandchildren. While he has developed close friendships with women and men in his community, his goal is to continue to make the grandkids his number-one priority.

When people lose a spouse or partner, they may look to create stronger ties with their siblings, even if they weren't close as children.

Amy and Julie lived three thousand miles apart, and they had different occupations and interests. Julie lived in New York City, was divorced, and worked as a waitress in Manhattan. Amy was a psychologist and was married to a doctor, William.

William died suddenly of an infection after heart surgery, about two months after Amy and Julie's mother passed away from cancer. At that time, Amy was forty-eight. Their father had died ten years earlier, and while both women felt a significant loss after losing both of their parents, they hadn't been particularly close with their mother.

While they were growing up, the two sisters, who were about fourteen years apart, had separate social circles and interests. Amy, the older sister, saw Julie, at most, once a year during annual family gatherings after Amy left home to go to college and graduate school. They got along okay with each other but didn't have much in common and drifted apart. Neither had any children.

When Amy's husband died, Amy's loss was compounded by the death of her mother. Amy mourned her husband and the relationship that she'd wanted to have with her mom but never nurtured. She had no cousins, parents, aunts, uncles, children, nieces, or nephews. Amy felt abandoned and distraught and began to realize that Julie must have experienced some of the same emotions when she divorced Hank.

Amy gradually became aware that Julie was her connection to the past, and she wanted to explore that relationship further and try to improve it. She invited

Julie to go with her on a cruise to Alaska. The sisters traveled together and tried to make up for lost time.

In the past, Amy had been too quick to judge Julie for having less-ambitious career goals. Now she recognized that Julie had dropped out of college to help their father, who was chronically ill. Julie worked as a waitress part-time so that she could assist the family. When caring for the family became too intense for Julie's husband, he simply left her.

Meanwhile, Julie resented the fact that Amy had the opportunity to go to college and pursue a prestigious career, an option that wasn't available to Julie because of her obligations to her parents.

On their trip, Julie discovered that although her sister wasn't physically present to take care of their parents, Amy worked overtime to send her mother money to support the family. As they shared their perspectives, each sister became more aware of the other's motivations, and they became more sympathetic and supportive of each other.

Eventually, Julie moved to an apartment near Amy and finished her remaining two years of college. The two sisters helped each other to heal from their losses. Julie met a wonderful man, remarried, and adopted a son. Amy found great joy in her new role as an aunt. They both regretted that their parents never got to see that they had become close, but they were grateful that they had rediscovered each other.

> As they shared their perspectives, each sister became more aware of the other's motivations, and they became more sympathetic and supportive of each other.

One of the biggest challenges that you'll face after losing your loved one is coping with loneliness. Your close relatives may live far away. You may not be interested in pursuing another coupled relationship. You might have health limitations that impact your ability to engage in activities that once brought you joy, like hiking, swimming, cycling, or painting.

What can you do to feel fulfilled and connected again? Consider building upon your existing friendships and reaching out to meet new people. After all, many people are in a similar situation to yours, and they have the same needs for friendship. This is why it's important to feel part of a community, and you can make that happen by living in the place that best fits your needs.

If you have children, think about what it was like when you were raising a family and the choices you made. For example, Paul and I relocated to Santa Cruz County from Los Angeles when Laura was in the fourth grade. We wanted to find a new home in a community with good schools and other families raising children.

We chose Scotts Valley, a suburb that was within a convenient driving distance of San Jose, where we both found jobs. What made this community so special was that our neighbors were like us. They moved there with the same goals as we had, and over time, we became good friends. To this day, more than twenty years later, many of my former neighbors still gather as a group once a month and on special occasions. When Paul was sick, they cooked for me and my family, ran errands for us, and continued to be there for me long after he died. Over the years, we've looked after each other.

My neighborhood friends were like my family, and that's the same type of friendships you can develop, even later in life. They can be people from your place of worship who gather for group activities. Or they can people that regularly attend your exercise class. If you live in a senior community, you may be surrounded by people in a situation very similar to yours. This can provide opportunities to participate in local activities, meet for coffee or tea, take a class, exercise together, and much more. These relationships can give you something to look forward to each day.

In addition to the new people you can meet, you may have long-term friends who have played an important role in your life. They also may have lost a spouse or partner. Continue to cultivate the relationships with those people who give you joy. They are your connection with the past and can play an important role in the future.

Learning to love again can mean different things to each individual. This can involve discovering a new relationship or expanding your career or personal goals. It can also include other ways to experience joy through the company of family, friends, and pets.

CHAPTER 8

▼

CONCLUSION

When you first lose your spouse or partner, it may be very difficult to think that you'll ever be able to experience joy again. Dealing with the loss, especially if it was unexpected, can be overwhelming. Handling even the most basic daily activities can seem impossible. By carefully working through your grief journey, getting help when you need it, and setting incrementally achievable goals, you can rebuild your life and find happiness again.

You don't have to heal alone. Contact your local hospice and sign up for one-on-one sessions or a grief support group. It's important to talk about your emotions and challenges as you work your way through loss. Grief groups, for example, offer a safe, nonjudgmental, supportive environment for sharing and healing.

Many hospices offer sessions for widows, widowers, and partners, as well as their families. Some hospices make these services available to everyone in their community and not just families of hospice patients. If you have children who are grieving, consider getting them help as well. There are specialized programs available to children, including camping experiences, art therapy, and other activities.

Follow the healing approach that works best for you. Depending on your situation, you may decide to see a therapist too. There is no standard time frame for being over grief, but you can rediscover a new-normal state with exciting opportunities you may have never imagined. This can include starting a new career, following a creative passion, doing volunteer work that gives you satisfaction, building new friendships, and becoming closer to people who are important to you. Based on your objectives, you may even find true love again. It's all up to you.

▼

A Close Look at the
First Year after Loss

UNDERSTANDING GRIEF—YOU'RE
NOT GOING CRAZY

Everyone's experience with grief is unique, and grieving isn't done all at once. There's no right or wrong way to cope with loss. In fact, you may experience many different emotions at the same time, such as sadness, anger, confusion, and guilt. Having these different emotions is normal, so go easy on yourself.

A lot has changed in grief-support strategies since Elisabeth Kubler-Ross identified the stages of grief in her book, *On Death and Dying*, published in 1969. She identified the following stages of grief: denial, anger, bargaining, depression, and acceptance.

These stages don't occur in any particular order. Not everyone experiences all of them, and sometimes people go back and forth from one stage to another. The Kubler-Ross approach was originally designed to help dying patients and later evolved as a model for survivors.

Over time, however, the Kubler-Ross model has been modified by many people in the grief-support community to focus more on tending to grief. This involves working through a variety of tasks related to accepting the reality of the loss, experiencing the pain of grief, and adjusting to living without that person while still maintaining a connection with your deceased loved one. I'll discuss an interpretation of this new model and how it can help you.

If your spouse or partner was terminally ill or had another very serious medical problem, you may have also experienced what's known as *anticipatory grief* before that person died. Anticipatory grief, just like grief after loss, can cause you to be distracted and to have trouble making decisions and concentrating. You may struggle with basic tasks, experience sleeplessness, and overeat or under-eat. It can lead to behaviors that aren't normal for you. That's why, for many people, the grief process begins long before their loved one dies. For example, it may start when their partners are diagnosed with a terminal illness or debilitating disease or when they exhibit signs of dementia.

As you work your way through the grief journey, particularly if you have the help of a grief-support expert, grief group, or therapist, it should become easier to accept the reality of the loss. While you still will experience the pain of grief, you'll discover that it may diminish over time. Of course, certain triggers can cause you to temporarily move a few steps back, just as you're trying to move forward. You'll learn how to adapt to your circumstances without your loved one and find a way to maintain the memories of that person. You can do this while beginning a new life and adjusting to what has become the "new normal."

Grief after a loss may begin with denying the reality of death, but working through the tasks of grief is not a linear process. I'll review some examples to help you understand how grief could be impacting you. It's common to experience moving back and forth from one emotion to another as you go through the different tasks.

Denial and Shock in Accepting the Reality of the Loss

Denial helps cushion you from dealing with too much grief all at once. Even if your loved one had cancer or another illness, and you thought you were prepared for the loss, it's still a shock when the death finally occurs. This feels surreal, and you likely will not be fully prepared for the emotions you might experience.

In many ways, if your loved one is no longer suffering, his or her passing may be a relief, although you may still feel lonely and empty. The loss can be so significant that you may develop certain practices to connect with that person.

For a brief time after his death, I kept Paul's cell phone line active and called it each night before I went to bed, just to listen to his voice mail message. I could've simply kept a recording of his voice, but somehow, I felt more connected to him by actually dialing his phone number. While I know this wasn't logical, I convinced myself that if I could hear his voice, then he was still with me. I needed to hold on to something that was familiar. For me, it was his voice. One night at 2:00 a.m., I dialed the wrong number, and a man answered the phone and said hello. It shook me up so much that I decided it was time to close Paul's cell phone account.

When I was particularly lonely, especially on our anniversary or his birthday, I would watch old videos of Paul. They made me cry, but I watched them anyway.

I also found it very difficult going to sleep because Paul was no longer next to me. So I took his framed picture and placed it on the pillow where he used to sleep, and I kissed it good night every evening. When my dog knocked the picture off the bed, I decided it was time to put that picture away too. I began to keep a journal—my nightly letter to Paul.

The process of journaling is very healing. I have described it in chapter 1. It helped me do what was necessary to break out of the denial phase.

Another ritual that people told me about is sleeping with their spouses' or partners' shirts, one that has not been washed, because the scent can be comforting. I didn't fully understand this concept until I got a puppy, Max, from my son Michael his wonderful wife, Kali. I was given the blanket that belonged to Max's mother and was told to keep it in Max's bedding so that he would be comforted by her scent as he transitioned from being part of the dog pack to joining us in his new home. Sure enough, he was very calm and slept comfortably from the start because he had his mommy's blanket.

Many people have told me that they walk through their homes and have brief but frequent one-way conversations with their deceased partners. They find this form of communication to be comforting. These conversations may go on for an extended period or crop up infrequently, many years later.

Their friends, who may not have experienced such a loss, are often bewildered when they learn about this type of communication or the other rituals I've discussed. They may seem to be judgmental and do not understand how this form of communication can be helpful and normal. Don't let their concerns discourage you from finding ways to help you cope, even if these approaches appear unconventional to others.

Denial and shock are very common when someone dies unexpectedly, such as from a sudden heart attack or accident, or when death is caused by a horrific circumstance, like an unforeseen suicide or murder. People who have watched their loved one suffer through a sudden death have the added burden of helplessness because they were present when it occurred, yet were unable to prevent this tragedy from happening.

This traumatic experience also applies if your loved one died, and you were the first person to find him or her. It takes time and effort to finally release these shocking images from your memory. By focusing on the positive memories of your spouse or partner, the traumatic and heartbreaking images can dissipate over time and may eventually disappear entirely.

If you've had to cope with a suicide, murder, or accident that you weren't able to prevent, the emotional loss is particularly devastating. The denial phase may last even longer than you'd expect. Grief support from a hospice organization can be very helpful, particularly beginning with one-on-one support before deciding whether you're ready to join a grief group. You also may greatly benefit by getting help from therapists, psychiatrists, and religious leaders. The trauma can be intense, and it may require multiple levels of support.

Experiencing Anger and Pain

Anger is a common reaction to the pain of grief, and shows its face in many ways. It's okay to be angry. You just lost the love of your life, and that's painful and scary. You may be angry at the doctors for not saving your spouse's life, or you could be angry at yourself for not being able to change the outcome.

When Paul died of cancer, I blamed myself for not having greater control over his diet. Because he loved to consume what most people would consider too much ice cream, cheese, and bread on a daily basis, I was convinced that I should have tried harder to convince him to follow a healthier diet.

I couldn't let go of my feelings of guilt until a grief counselor gave me sage advice: "He's an adult, and it was his choice to eat those types of foods. Plus, it's also unlikely that this diet caused his cancer." After hearing her reassuring words, I gave myself permission to stop being angry at myself for something that was out of my control and probably would not have made a difference.

Some people are angry at themselves because they weren't home when their spouses or partners died. Instead, they may have found their loved ones passed out on the floor, when it was too late to save them.

A common reaction is, "If only I had gotten home ten minutes earlier, I could have called an ambulance, and she'd be alive today." Or someone may have been present during the death and hopelessly watched a loved one had a heart attack. Even though the person called 911 immediately and attempted CPR, there was nothing else that could have changed the outcome. Or people may be angry at themselves for postponing the trips they wanted to take with their partners and other activities they put on hold because the responsibilities of work stood in the way.

You may be angry at your husband, wife, or partner for not taking better care of himself or herself, and you may feel that person somehow unwittingly contributed to the death. Perhaps your loved one refused to take the medication that the doctor recommended.

You may feel abandoned, and now you have to deal with the emotional and financial complexities associated with loss. You may be more likely to feel resentful if your spouse or partner spent too much time working or drinking and not enough time exercising, relaxing, and maintaining a healthy diet.

It's not unusual to be angry at the world and blame yourself, doctors, your spouse, a higher power, and lifestyle choices. While it's normal to feel this anger, there are ways to release it. See chapter 1 for helpful tips.

Dealing with Guilt, Regrets, and "If Onlys"

Feeling guilty and having regrets can happen before and after a loss. It's where the if-only and what-if statements are common. You may try to bargain with a higher power, saying, "What if I give up ten years of my life so that my partner can live?" You may explore hypothetical situations, like, "I'll do anything, God, if you just make my spouse live again." This is what Kubler-Ross called bargaining. Unfortunately, bargaining isn't an option once it becomes evident that there's no way to change a terminal diagnosis.

After the person dies, you may torment yourself by thinking about things you would do differently if you could simply change the past. It's where you might say:

- "If only I had taken him to another doctor and gotten better advice sooner, he might have lived."
- "If only I had been home when she had a heart attack, I could have saved her."

Sadly, some people spend years punishing themselves for not recognizing the signs of their partner's illnesses. They might ask themselves:

- "Why can't I have another chance with him?"
- "Why did I let her stay in a job that was stressful and that might have contributed to her early death?"

You may carry guilt and regrets with you after loss, but the loss must be dealt with and worked through. After all, you can't see the future, and you can't change the past. It's not your fault. Bad things happen to good people. Accidents and unfortunate situations occur. Illnesses are simply part of life. All you can do is focus on where you are now and determine how to learn from, cope with, or make positive changes as a result of this loss. Here are a few examples of how I transformed the insight from loss into positive experiences:

Long before Paul and I knew that he had cancer, we wanted to travel overseas, but we kept putting off the trip. Usually, our work schedules got in the way. Then we had unexpected bills that made it seem impractical to spend the money. There were always excuses to avoid traveling.

After Paul died, I blamed myself for not taking the vacations when we could have somehow made them possible by planning a shorter trip, using frequent-flyer miles, or staying at more reasonably priced places. Ultimately, I was able to release these regrets by giving myself permission to make time for travel after he died. I shared with my friends details about the vacations that we had planned but never took and how sad I was that I missed these opportunities. After listening to me, one couple immediately began saving for vacation, and now they regularly take an annual trip together, based on my advice.

Although I never went on that special trip with Paul, I traveled there with our girls a year after his death. Whenever possible, I tried to slow down, become more flexible, and savor precious moments with my family. That's easy to do when you're in a beautiful place and away from the day-to-day responsibilities that are part of your everyday routine at home. It's a lesson that grief teaches people. You only have so many days on this planet, so make the most of them.

Coping with Feelings of Sadness, Loneliness, and Depression

You have every right to feel sad, lonely, and depressed when you lose someone. Even the most optimistic people may experience feelings of depression as they deal with their grief.

You may feel sad, lonely, and depressed without being clinically depressed. What do these emotions look like? Mealtimes, which were once an opportunity to connect with your loved one, may no longer be enjoyable. Eating habits change, and looking forward to the daily routines of breakfast, lunch, and dinner may fade. Some people simply cut back on food. After all, there's less incentive to cook for just one person. They may be so sad that they don't even feel like eating. Other people compensate by overindulging in food or alcohol.

Doing things alone, like going to a fancy restaurant, movie, or play—activities that you may have enjoyed doing with your other half—can be potentially stressful and lonely until you're ready. I've known some people who rarely left their houses for many months after a loss, even when they were invited to gatherings by well-meaning friends.

Instead, they withdrew from engaging in outside experiences to the point that even going to the grocery store made them anxious. They might have been lonely, but they didn't have the emotional energy to reach out and connect with others. Other people either slept too much or, conversely, found it difficult to sleep.

You may find it challenging to make even the most basic decisions. You could have trouble deciding whether you should read the newspaper or let it remain on the kitchen table. You may leave weeks of mail or email unopened or fail to listen to or answer telephone calls because this requires too much emotional effort. For example, if you open the mail, you might find an unexpected bill that you're not prepared to deal with at the time.

It could be uncomfortable to talk to people, because even phone conversations can be overwhelming when you don't know how to respond when people ask you how you're doing. If you tell them you're not fine, they might ask probing questions that you don't want to answer. Even the simple act of taking a shower and changing out of your bathrobe, pajamas, or sweats can be a chore that you might put off for a few days.

When my father died unexpectedly of a heart attack, I looked at a pile of laundry a week later and thought, *How am I ever going to be able to wash this?* That was so unlike me at the time—I was a super-type-A person, who bragged about the ability to multitask my way through life. (That was the old me. I work at a much saner pace now.) So why did doing a simple, daily task like laundry suddenly seem so overwhelming? It was because I was unknowingly working my way through feelings of depression and being overwhelmed. The most basic chore seemed daunting at the time.

As I mentioned, everyone experiences grief differently. You may cry suddenly without knowing why. (That's why we have tissue boxes on hand at every grief group meeting). Perhaps more unsettling is *not* being able to cry because you're so sad that you can't release the pain. Even if you're not normally prone to experiencing extreme sadness or depression, you can generally expect to soften this pain that seems new to you. It may require therapy, medication, the passage of time, a change in your routine, or a combination of all these things.

If you were a caretaker for your spouse or partner, you were probably running on adrenaline for a long time and putting your own needs on hold. Taking care of that person may have been your full-time job. When your loved one is gone, your job as a caretaker is over. All of a sudden—particularly if you have retired, have your own health issues, or don't have much of a support network or other major responsibilities—you may feel extremely isolated and bereft. The job of being a caretaker kept you going, but it took a physical and emotional toll on you, which is often referred to as *caretaker fatigue*. That's why it's so important to give yourself permission to take the time necessary to get back to where you were, physically and emotionally, before the loss.

Accepting And Adjusting To Your New Life

There *is* light at the end of tunnel, although it may take time before you see it. Acceptance is where you finally come to terms with the fact that your loved one is not physically coming back. That paves the way for adjusting to a world without your partner. You may look in the closet, and his clothes are still there. Her picture may still be on the wall. His files and books may be scattered about the house, but the only place you'll see him is in your dreams.

Dreams can be comforting and help you through this transition period, but not everyone dreams about the deceased spouse. You may be in too much emotional pain to have these dreams, but if you can remember your dreams, they may help you to sort out your unconscious emotions.

I had many dreams for more than ten years after Paul's death. In them, he has returned, and I try to explain to him about all the changes in technology that he missed because he died in 2006. One of my favorite dreams is seeing him ring the doorbell, and I shout, "You're back! You're not going to believe all of the things you can do with the iPhone today." Then I show him how he can use it to take pictures or videos, do Facetime calls, and so much more. Of course, once I wake up, I realize that it was just another dream, but it brings a smile to my face.

By accepting the loss, you may understand that you'll need to deal with the new situation that has been forced upon you. While you still may talk about your spouse or partner in the present tense, it's time to think about how you can adjust to the sad reality that the one you love is no longer physically here.

As you begin to accept the loss, you may be ready to take mini-steps and set incremental goals that are manageable.

As you begin to accept the loss, you may be ready to take mini-steps and set incremental goals that are manageable. At that time, it's a good idea to visualize where you want to be over the next few years, and focus on your most critical priorities. Ultimately, when you come to terms with the fact that your loved one is gone, you can identify which actions to take to find happiness and fulfillment at this point in your life.

Unfortunately, some people can't seem to reach a level of acceptance and adjust to the new normal in a reasonable amount of time. There's no definition for what's considered reasonable, but after the first year people may be more likely to begin to accept the reality of their loss. Failure to adjust to the loss delays their ability to move forward. Here's an example that illustrates why acceptance is so important:

> Mark was unjustly irate at the staff who cared for his wife at a nursing home and blamed them for her death. He spent many years being angry and researched ways to sue them. Although he never took legal action against the facility, his anger continued to build. He wasn't able to see that the personnel did everything possible to keep his wife, Bella, comfortable and alive. The facility had an excellent rating, and the staff members were very attentive to Bella. Sadly, Mark couldn't accept the reality that Bella died because her heart was weak and eventually gave out.
>
> For twenty years, he lived with this anger. It continued to be part of Mark's conversations with his friends, who became weary of hearing the same old story repeatedly. Because Mark couldn't accept the terms of her death, it sapped a lot of his energy.
>
> The bottom line: If you want to avoid Mark's fate, try to accept and release the pain associated with things that can't be changed. If you can't do this on your own, consider getting therapy, grief support, or both.

At the other extreme is Nia, who not only accepted a loss in a reasonable amount of time but also used it as way to help others.

Nia got to know the people at the nursing home who took care of Ben, her partner. A few weeks after Ben passed away, Nia wrote a letter to the director of the facility, thanking them for keeping Ben as comfortable as possible. Nia accepted that Ben's time was limited due to his illness.

About two years after Ben died, Nia volunteered to teach a knitting class at the facility in appreciation of the staff's efforts. She was able to deal with grief in a positive manner, come to terms with her loss, and feel good about helping others at the same time.

Some people accept the loss, adjust to accommodate their loss, and then bounce back into feeling depressed, angry, sad, and guilty. Remember that with grief, you may take two steps forward and one step back. Set realistic expectations, but go easy on yourself when you backslide. You've been through a lot. Be patient, and expect relapses. This is normal.

Some of your friends may feel awkward when dealing with the topic of loss, and they may unknowingly say things that can be hurtful. Their comments are not meant to hurt you. They just lack your perspective.

People who haven't lost loved ones don't always understand that grief comes in waves. They may not be aware of the impact of the new normal that you are experiencing. They may not realize how disturbing it is to hear someone say, "It has been many months. I thought you'd be done grieving by now." Be open with your friends, and kindly ask them to refrain from judging you. Let them know that you are still tending to your grief and that you're moving at your own pace.

As I've discussed, people process grief in their own unique way, and there's no set timeline for grief. It might be easier to move forward after you get through the first year because you'll know that you made it through those difficult milestones—birthdays, anniversaries, and holidays. For some people, though, the first year is such a blur that the reality of the loss doesn't sink in until later, and so they do their grief work in the second year and beyond.

Your friends and family members may be reluctant to mention your loved one because they don't know how this could impact you. They may not realize that part of working through grief is in sharing stories and happy moments and in talking about what made your partner so wonderful. By sharing your experiences, the good memories come to the surface, and eventually, the traumatic images of watching a loved one waste away from cancer or another type of debilitating condition fade away. Over time, the images are generally replaced with the memories of when the person was vibrant and healthy.

In my personal experience, I no longer remember what Paul looked like when he was dying and had lost sixty pounds in a short time. When I think of him, the only image that comes to mind is that of a healthy, happy man.

IDENTIFYING COMMON REACTIONS TO GRIEF

When you are grieving, you may experience different emotions at once and may become easily distracted. The way you deal with people socially may change. You may find yourself talking to your deceased loved one and be more likely to question and worry about your own mortality.

How do you determine if some of the problems you are dealing with stem from grief, stress, or other challenges that you are facing? I often share the following resource with people in grief groups and with friends who have lost loved ones to give them insight into what's happening. It's from "The Journey of Grief" by Hospice of Santa Cruz County. The information in the chart helps people to realize that the emotions they are experiencing, along with changes in how they interact with people and their environment, are normal. Look closely, and see how it relates to your experience.

Tip

Physically, you may experience:	Many different emotions can be felt at once:	Your thoughts may include:
• Exhaustion • Emptiness in stomach • Tightness in chest • Shortness of breath • Dry mouth • Increased noise sensitivity • Appetite changes • Sleep disturbances • Low motivation	• Sadness • Loneliness • Anger • Guilt • Anxiety • Shock • Relief • Numbness • Depression • Sudden crying • Fear • Helplessness	• Disbelief • Distraction • Absentmindedness • Forgetfulness • Dreaming of him or her • Poor concentration • Memories of other losses • Denial • Diminished self-concern
Socially, you may feel: • A need to withdraw • Less desire to converse • A need to take care of others	Your actions may include: • Carrying special objects • Crying • Visiting the gravesite • Talking to the person who died	Spiritual questions may come up: • What will happen to me when I die? • Where is he/she now? • How could God allow this? • When will I die?

Common Grief Reactions
(Source: *Journey of Grief,* Hospice of Santa Cruz County)

Look at this chart whenever you have doubts about why you may be distracted or why your reactions to people and situations are much different than before you were faced with the loss. It will help you to realize that what you're experiencing may be due to grief. Many of these emotions and reactions will diminish over time as you begin to heal.

EXPLORING A GRIEF TIMELINE—
DEALING WITH MULTIPLE LOSSES

Multiple losses compound and create complex grief. If you haven't fully worked through the prior losses of friends and family members who have passed, then it will be much more challenging to deal with your current loss.

I attended a workshop in which Alexandra Kennedy, a licensed marriage and family therapist and author, discussed the concept of creating a grief timeline, which can help you to understand how the death of important people in your life has impacted you. She also discusses a timeline in detail in her books, *Honoring Grief* and *The Infinite Thread: Healing Relationships Beyond Loss.*

Reconstructing a timeline gives you the opportunity to explore how you reacted to those losses. I'll use my own family as an example:

Sample Grief Timeline

- Early 1960s: My young cousin, Robbie, died of leukemia. I was just a child, and we got a phone call that he was gone. There was no fanfare. One day he was here; the next day he was not. I missed Robbie but never fully understood the impact of this loss until much later in life.

- Mid-1960s: My grandparents on my father's side both died about a week apart. No one talked about my grandparents except to say they were gone. I was sad, but there wasn't really any closure. I was just told that they were old and sick and that their deaths were to be expected.

- Mid-1970s: My grandfather on my mother's side died of a heart attack. By then, I was an adult and had gotten to know him. I saw him in the hospital before he died and got to say goodbye. For the first time in my family, death wasn't glossed over. I attended his funeral and had a few dreams about him after his passing.

• Early 1980s: My grandmother on my mother's side died of a heart attack, and this death really hit me hard. I was very close to her, saw her frequently, and recently had made plans to go out to lunch with her the week of her death. I had dreams about her for several months after her death and thought about her often. I never got therapy or grief support for the loss. I just kept on going.

• Late 1980s: One of the worst days of my life occurred when my fifty-seven-year-old father died of a sudden heart attack while on vacation with my mom and my two boys. It was such a shock. Although I was married and had a wonderful husband and family, I had no idea how I would cope with the loss of my father. I somehow managed to keep myself together to help organize his service and deliver the eulogy.

I never went to grief counseling or had therapy at the time. I just assumed that when someone dies, you have to be brave and move on quickly. For many years, I tried to connect with him in my dreams. I thought about him at night and imagined that he was still present and guiding me in my thoughts. It was very hard to accept his death. I was so focused on my own loss of my father that I didn't even realize what my mother or sons were going through.

My sons had to witness their grandpa dying in front of them. Along with my mom, they experienced not being able to do anything to save him. None of us got the help we needed, which could have made it easier to deal with this loss. Instead, my family and I just threw ourselves into activities so that we didn't have to face or deal with the pain.

My mom and I were both workaholics, so we just loaded up on projects and stayed busy. I told my sons that it was very sad that their grandfather died, but we didn't talk about it very much. In retrospect, I realize that I didn't get the support needed to understand how this loss could have impacted them.

- Late '90s: My father-in-law, Paul's dad, died after a long illness. I was prepared for his death because we knew he had been sick, but of course I was saddened by the loss. We had closure with a funeral and the support of family members. I worried about the impact this had on Paul's mom, Paul, his brothers, and other family members.

- 2006: Paul was diagnosed with cancer in November 2005 and died in less than six months. This time, I was better prepared than when I lost my father. With the help of hospice, a social worker was available who addressed my anticipatory grief issues as Paul's health became progressively worse. After his death, I attended one-on-one sessions and a grief group. Laura and Megan got counseling. When Paul died, I became more aware of the grief process, and I thought about the loss of my father and how that had impacted my life.

- 2018: My mom had remarried more than ten years after my dad passed away, and her husband, my stepfather, died suddenly in the hospital. It was a shock, and I was saddened. Because I understood the grief process by that time, I was able to console his children, my mom, and other family members.

Developing a loss timeline helped me to realize that if I could get through one loss, I could deal with another. But it also made me aware that if I didn't take the time to fully mourn a previous loss, it would make dealing with my current one more challenging. This also reinforces why grief support is so important and how therapy also can help.

The timeline described here relates only to losing someone by death. If you add in other losses, like financial disasters, losing a job, or having your own serious health issue, it can compound your grief.

If you're far enough along in your grief journey that you feel comfortable developing your own timeline, then give it a try, based on the directions below. If this is too painful right now, skip this step.

How to Create a Grief Timeline

1. List the key losses you've had over time and how you handled them.
2. Go back and identify any loss where you didn't take the time needed to mourn it.
3. Determine what you'd do differently, based on what you know now.
4. If you have any prior losses that are unresolved and interfering with your ability to deal with the loss of your spouse or partner, determine what you can do to help release those feelings. For example, if your mother died within a short time after losing your husband, think about how to apply some of the principles in this book to help you have the emotional space to deal with both losses.

You'll be surprised at what you'll learn when you complete a timeline and see how your prior losses are affecting you. By understanding the grief process and common reactions to it, you can get a better perspective on what's causing you the most pain and how to soothe it.

COPING DURING THE FIRST YEAR

This is when the loss begins to sink in. The first few months may be such a blur that you rarely remember some of the new people you meet. You may keep thinking that you'll wake up from this bad dream, and your partner will appear next to you. Sorting through your partner's possessions can be so painful that you may put it off for many months. You may look at other couples and think, *Why do they get to have a partner, and I don't?*

Go easy on yourself, especially in the beginning. Don't try to tackle too many tasks at once. You not only miss this person, but you may also have to take care of the responsibilities that your loved one handled, which adds to your workload and stress. As a result, you may discover in the first few months that you can accomplish only about half of what you usually can do.

When friends or family members offer to help with things like chores, errands, and meals, take them up on their offers, and don't feel that you need to reciprocate right now. You may want someone to be with you as you sort through your partner's belongings or to move them to a place where you can go through them later, like in a garage.

If people want to bring you meals, let them. If they invite you to dinner at their homes, attend, if you're ready. If you're too tired to walk your dog, let the kids in your neighborhood do this for you. People want to help, and these are some of the ways they can make your life easier.

What are some other changes you might notice the first year? Some people say that they talk out loud to their loved ones, ask questions, and hope that the answers will come to them in their dreams. Of course, that's assuming they're able to sleep. As I mentioned earlier, eating habits may change too. You may look at food differently than before. Eating may be something that you do just to stay alive instead of getting enjoyment from a delicious meal. Some people may go the other extreme and overeat to satisfy a craving for an immediate reward.

What are some strategies that can help you deal with the desire to communicate with your loved one? How can you maintain a healthy lifestyle by eating three wholesome meals a day and getting a good night's sleep?

Accept the fact that it's normal to want to connect with and hear from your partner or spouse. Do whatever makes you feel comfortable. In chapter 1, I discussed that journaling is a good way to express your feelings and can help you transition to the changes that you're experiencing as a result of this loss. Some people write in a journal for months, while others may take much longer. Eventually, you may decide to jot down thoughts only when the mood strikes you, rather than on a regular basis.

Some people find comfort in going through photo albums or old letters or watching videos of their spouses or partners whenever they feel a strong need for that connection. I watched videos of Paul periodically over the first few years. Sometimes they made me feel better, but they'd also often make me cry.

Maintaining sensible eating patterns are a big challenge to people after loss. One widow I know ate only one meal a day for many months, except when she was with other people. This disrupted her well-being, and she became lethargic, irritable, and weak. It wasn't until her doctor warned her of the dangers of not maintaining a healthy diet that she began to eat regular meals again and regain her health.

At the other end of the spectrum, a widower, who had always been at an ideal weight, starting gorging on pizza and dessert and drinking excessively to feel better. It wasn't until his children commented on his sudden weight gain that he decided to take dieting and exercising seriously. Losing someone takes a physical toll on your body, so please go that extra mile and focus on healthy habits.

Sleeping is particularly difficult for many people.

One woman, Jill, told me that she rarely fell asleep before 3:00 a.m. because she felt too sad to go to bed without her husband. So she watched TV, including the news and murder mysteries, and spent evenings on her computer, long after she should have gone to sleep. Jill wound up sleeping late each morning and was out of sync with the schedules of her friends, family, and part-time work obligations.

Eventually, she visited a therapist who recommended that Jill take a mild sleeping pill until she was able to maintain normal sleeping habits and change her evening routine. After several months, Jill was able to make changes that made it easier for her to sleep at night. She reduced her caffeine consumption to just one cup of coffee in the morning, exercised daily, and read a magazine or book or sections from the Bible before going to bed.

Also, consider watching something on TV other than the news if you have trouble sleeping. Typical newscasts are frequently filled with negative information—who got killed in an accident or murder, how politics can disrupt your life, how natural disasters are causing people to lose their homes, and so on.

Don't get me wrong; I think it's important to know what's going on in your community and the world. In fact, very early in my career, I was a journalist and worked in radio and TV news. I've noticed, however, that watching the news late at night and learning about the problems going on in the world can be troubling.

Having a positive, calming routine makes it easier to sleep. Think about the approaches people take to get a baby to sleep. I'll bet it doesn't include shouting matches on TV and stories that are disturbing.

Even the most organized person will likely notice the struggle it takes to get organized at a time when the loss is overwhelming. There are so many things to be done—papers to fill out, accounts to sort through, people to contact, and decisions to make. Where do you even begin? You may want to make radical changes in your life and find yourself making impulsive decisions. Or you could be completely avoiding making decisions about even the most basic tasks because you don't want to cope with one more responsibility or change.

Developing Priorities and Goals

What are some approaches to taking control when you feel overwhelmed? Make a list of your top priorities and goals. Think about what you want to accomplish by the end of the year and how to you plan to get there. This involves understanding your big-picture goals and then setting incremental ones for each month. You can always work on longer-range goals later.

Use a day planner (or a calendar on your smartphone or computer) and update it periodically with things that you want to accomplish and dates to get them done. (Call me old-school, but I prefer to track things on my day planner instead of my phone's calendar.) Each night before you go to bed, review what you plan to do the next day. You may modify the list, but this approach gives you the opportunity to chart your progress and hold yourself accountable.

Here's an example of priorities and goals to consider:

Sample Top Priorities for the First Year

- Stay mentally and physically healthy.
- Visit with friends and family more often.
- Take control of finances, and develop a financial plan.
- Don't accept more work than you can handle.
- Take a music class, and join a local choir.
- Identify what makes you happy, gives you something to look forward to, and gives you hope.
- Travel with a friend.

Here's an example of goals for a particular month and how to break them down:

Sample Monthly Goal

- See your doctor for a checkup, and get on a regular eating schedule.
- Clean out George's closet and give away items to friends and charities.
- Seek professional help to deal with loss, either a therapist or grief counseling from hospice.
- Exercise three times a week.
- Visit with a friend at least once a week.
- Organize paperwork and automate payments for bills.
- Plan a trip.
- Investigate music classes.

Here are some of the types of items that you can add to your daily checklist. Don't try to add too many tasks in a single day. Keep the list manageable.

Sample Daily Checklist

- Make an appointment to see your doctor.
- Go to a yoga class.
- Review bill payments.
- Have lunch with Susan.
- Buy groceries.

Goal-setting is so important. If you haven't identified your priorities and a path for achieving them, each day can run into the next and leave you feeling like you haven't accomplished anything. That emotion can trigger a cycle of hopelessness.

Make Taking Care of Your Health a Big Priority

When Paul died, I knew that I needed to make the most of each day and do whatever I could to stay healthy, not just for myself but also for my family. Like many caretakers, I put my own checkups on hold when he was sick because I didn't have time to visit a doctor.

My focus had been on getting through each day and making sure I did whatever was needed to help Paul. His illness took a physical toll on me. My hair started falling out in clumps due to the stress. My eating habits were irregular.

After he died, I got back into exercising on a regular basis. I tried to eat three balanced meals a day, even when I didn't feel like eating. I did the necessary follow-up visits with doctors. Death makes you realize how fleeting life is. When you make your health a priority, you can be better prepared to handle whatever other challenges and opportunities come your way.

Developing Coping Strategies

Losing someone can impact you physically. You may feel weak or tired. Stomach problems and headaches from the stress of loss are very common. Perhaps you put off seeing a doctor for your own health matters while taking care of your loved one, and now you dread having to visit a doctor for yourself. Going to a medical office again can bring back painful memories. Plus, you may be afraid that you'll get bad health news. If you have concerns, enlist a friend or family member to be with you at your medical appointment.

After the first few months following your spouse's or partner's death, the outpouring of help from people may subside. You're often left to deal with the aftermath on your own. People who haven't been through this type of loss may not realize how difficult this is for you. You eventually need to learn how to adapt and accept the new normal, and try not to let comments from others cause you additional pain.

For example, Marge, a widow, was invited to attend the wedding anniversary of good friends shortly after the death of her husband. She was seated at a table of married people. When the music started, and everyone else got up to dance, Marge realized that she was alone. This made her feel sad and frightened. Marge also wasn't invited to dinner events with friends that she used to visit with when she was married. It dawned on Marge that she was being pushed into a world of singles, and she needed to accept her new status.

Tip

This book explains how holidays, anniversaries, and birthdays, which were once so joyous, can turn into events that you might dread, unless you're prepared. When you have a plan B for these events, and you get through the first year, you are more likely to adjust better to these events in the following years. But dealing with these emotional triggers can be a challenge. Think about what would make you most comfortable during these times, and make plans that will help you. This can include the following:

- Surround yourself with family and/or friends during holidays and special events.
- Change your traditional holiday experiences, such as visiting new places, lightening your burden if you normally do the hosting, or volunteering at a soup kitchen or your local place of worship.
- Have a birthday party honoring your loved one.
- Be with a friend or family members on your wedding anniversary or do a ritual that will give you comfort, such as taking a walk along his favorite hiking trail, watching her favorite TV show, or preparing a special meal.

As you go through the year, look at your priorities and goals periodically, and see how well you've done. You may need to make some adjustments and possibly take a few things off the list if your goals were too ambitious. I always mention to the people who attend grief groups that they should be proud they were able to leave the comfort of their homes and that they found the courage to show up each week and share their stories and grief with the group. It's a big step and commitment to say, "I want some help in dealing with this loss, and I'm willing to make the effort to get it."

When you went from *we* to *me*, your social circle likely changed. If you made a few new friends, give yourself credit for taking the initiative and reaching out.

Perhaps you had many sleepless nights after the loss and ate at irregular times. If, by the end of the year, you're able to sleep much better and have established a structure for healthy eating and sleeping habits, congratulate yourself for taking those important steps.

I was surprised to find that many women of the Silent Generation—parents of the baby boomers—found themselves paying bills and making important financial decisions for the first time in their lives after their loss. It was a big leap for some women in their eighties, who had been homemakers, to suddenly learn how to take on new responsibilities and adapt to technology.

Keep in mind that TV wasn't even invented when they were born, yet they may have had to adjust to electronic bill paying, dealing with email issues, and making online purchases. I encourage these people to get outside help whenever necessary. They may get this help from their grandkids. My own grandkids have taught me things about downloading apps that I wasn't even aware of, and I consider myself to be tech-savvy.

Similarly, some of the older men might need to learn how to make meals and do laundry. Men also may have struggled with technology, but maybe their wives or partners had mastered how to use a computer. When their wives died, these men had to learn new skills or get outside help.

Ultimately, I've seen how these men and women have stepped up, evolved, and moved forward by learning basic but critical tasks that had been done by their spouses or partners.

What changes can you expect by the end of first year? Change happens incrementally, and each step puts you closer to healing. Some people—depending on their situations—became comfortable with socializing in new groups. Others got closer to their old friends and family but also reached out to meet new people. Women who never had been to upscale restaurants on their own or who had never seen a movie alone discovered that the experience was enjoyable.

Many of these people met new friends in their grief groups and continued those friendships after the group ended. As a general rule, after a year you will have encountered various challenges, but you will gradually make some inroads into dealing with the realities of your loss.

ACKNOWLEDGMENTS

I'd like to recognize Paul for his courage and love. If he were alive today, he'd say, "This a good book, but isn't there anything you can do to add some humor to it?" I know this because I gave him a copy of his eulogy to review months before he died. He sent it back for editing a few times until I added enough anecdotes to make him happy.

Of course, I'd like to thank my entire family, which also includes Paul's relatives, for their support, guidance, and love as they've helped me to rebuild my life after loss. My family has expanded over the years, and it has been a blessing to welcome each new member—spouses, grandchildren, and more. Jack's relatives have also been a wonderful new addition to my life.

I want to particularly recognize Jack, my remarkable husband, who has shown me how it's possible to find true love again. Many thanks also go to my fantastic friends, who were always there for me.

I'd also like to thank Hospice of Santa Cruz County for giving me the opportunity to provide grief support to others. I'd particularly like to recognize the following people from that hospice: Cathy Conway, Chief Mission Officer; Cindi Gray, Director of Grief Support; and Margaret Gordon, board member. They provided valuable feedback and insight to help make this book possible.

I really appreciate the guidance from Alexandra Kennedy, a licensed marriage and family therapist and author. She patiently reviewed multiple iterations of this book and helped me to organize and focus the content in a manner that will be the most valuable, based on where people are in their grief journey. Her books—*Honoring Grief,*

Losing a Parent, and *The Infinite Thread: Healing Relationships Beyond Loss*—are all excellent resources for helping people to deal with loss and find happiness and meaning in their lives.

My friend Alesa Lightbourne, award-winning author of *The Kurdish Bike*, has given me valuable insight to make the book more compelling.

I'd also like to recognize other dedicated reviewers who provided excellent feedback for the book:

- Albert Berman
- Myra Berman
- Barbara Colella
- Dawn Donovan
- Rosalind Hain
- Paul Karz
- Margie Lafia
- Deborah Malkin
- Patti Schlunt
- Pilar Straw

When I began working on *After Loss*, I originally intended to write it just for women. I'm grateful to my friend's son, Ross, who suggested that the book should also focus on men who have experienced loss.

Made in the USA
San Bernardino, CA
05 September 2019